International Institute for the Unification of Private Law (UNIDROIT)

International Institute for the Unification of Private Law (UNIDROIT)

Fourth Edition

Lena Peters

This book was originally published as a monograph in the International Encyclopaedia of Laws/Intergovernmental Organizations.

Founding Editor: Roger Blanpain
General Editor: Frank Hendrickx
Volume Editor: Jan Wouters

Wolters Kluwer

Published by:
Kluwer Law International B.V.
PO Box 316
2400 AH Alphen aan den Rijn
The Netherlands
E-mail: lrs-sales@wolterskluwer.com
Website: www.wolterskluwer.com/en/solutions/kluwerlawinternational

Sold and distributed by:
Wolters Kluwer Legal & Regulatory U.S.
920 Links Avenue
Landisville, PA 17538
United States of America
E-mail: customer.service@wolterskluwer.com

Printed on acid-free paper

ISBN 978-94-035-1557-1

e-Book: ISBN 978-94-035-1567-0
web-PDF: ISBN 978-94-035-1577-9

This title is available on www.kluwerlawonline.com

The Author

A Swedish national, Ms Lena Peters grew up in Italy where she attended an English school. In 1978, she took her *Juris Kandidatexamen* at Stockholm University followed by a Master of Laws from King's College, London (1979). From 1985 to 2023, she was with the International Institute for the Unification of Private Law, more commonly known as UNIDROIT, first as Research Officer, lastly as Principal Legal Officer. From 1986 to 1994, she was Secretary to the Working Group for the Preparation of Principles of International Commercial Contracts, from 1994 to 2000 Secretary to the Study Group on Franchising and from 2001 to 2002 Secretary to the Committee of Governmental Experts on Franchising. She also collaborated on the project for the preparation of the ELI-UNIDROIT Model European Rules of Civil Procedure. From 2013 to 2023, she was responsible for the publications of the organization. In June 2023, she retired but will continue to collaborate with the organization as Managing Editor of the *Uniform Law Review*, a position she has held since January 2013.

This monograph draws upon UNIDROIT documents and publications, both electronic and paper-based. The author wishes to express her thanks to the organization for permission to quote and draw from UNIDROIT materials.

The Author

Table of Contents

Table of Contents

List of Abbreviations

ALI	American Law Institute
APG	Aircraft Protocol Group
AWG	Aviation Working Group
CIM 1970	International Convention Concerning the Carriage of Goods by Rail
CISG 1980	United Nations Convention on Contracts for the International Sale of Goods
CMR 1956	Geneva Convention on the Contract for the International Carriage of Goods by Road (*Convention du 1956 relative au contrat de transport international de marchandises par route)*
CRTD 1989	Convention on Civil Liability for Damage Caused During Carriage of Dangerous Goods by Road, Rail and Inland Navigation Vessels
DLT	Distributed Ledger Technology
ECE	United Nations Economic Commission for Europe
ELI	European Law Institute
EU	European Union
FAO	Food and Agriculture Organization of the United Nations
HCCH	Hague Conference on Private International Law
IAEA	International Atomic Energy Agency
IATA	International Air Transport Association
IBA	International Bar Association
ICAO	International Civil Aviation Organization
ICC	International Chamber of Commerce
IDLO	International Development Law Organization
IFAD	International Fund for Agricultural Development
ILO	International Labour Organization

List of Abbreviations

IMO	International Maritime Organization
IRU	International Road Transport Union
ISDA	International Derivatives Association
OAS	Organization of American States
OECD	Organisation for Economic Co-operation and Development
OHBLA	Organisation for the Harmonisation of Business Law in Africa (*OHADA –Organisation pour l'harmonisation en Afrique du droit des affaires*)
OTIF	Intergovernmental Organisation for International Carriage by Rail (*Organisation intergouvernementale pour les transports internationaux ferroviaires*)
OTT 1991	Convention of the Liability of Operators of Transport Terminals
RWG	Rail Working Group
SWG	Space Working Group
ULFC 1964	Convention relating to a Uniform Law on the Formation of Contracts for the International Sale of Goods
ULIS 1964	Convention relating to a Uniform Law on the International Sale of Goods
UNCITRAL	United Nations Commission on International Trade Law
UNESCO	United Nations Organization for Education, Science and Culture
UNIDROIT	International Institute for the Unification of Private Law
UNILEX	Data Base on CISG and the UNIDROIT Principles of the Centre for Comparative and Foreign Law Studies
UNOOSA	United Nations Office for Outer Space Affairs
WIPO	World Intellectual Property Organization

Part I. Genesis and Historical Development

1. Law is an integral part of the activities of most international organizations, be they universal, multilateral or regional. Thus, organizations as diverse as the International Civil Aviation Organization (ICAO), the International Maritime Organization (IMO), the World Intellectual Property Organization (WIPO), the Food and Agriculture Organization of the United Nations (FAO), the International Atomic Energy Agency (IAEA), and the Organisation for Economic Co-operation and Development (OECD) all have departments or divisions that deal with the legal aspects of their activities. Regional organizations such as the Council of Europe, the European Union (EU), the MERCOSUR, and the Organization of American States (OAS) or the Organization for the Harmonization of Business Law in Africa (OHBLA)[1] are no different. But only a very few deal exclusively with law: the Hague Conference on Private International Law (HCCH) which specializes in private international law or conflict of laws, the United Nations Commission on International Trade Law (UNCITRAL), which is a Commission of the United Nations and specializes in commercial law, and UNIDROIT, which this contribution will examine in greater detail.

2. The origins of UNIDROIT date back to the first decades of the twentieth century.[2] It was on 26 September 1924 that the Assembly of the League of Nations was called upon to take a decision in relation to an offer made by the Italian Government following an initiative by Senator Vittorio Scialoja, Professor of Roman Law at the University of Rome, for the establishing in Rome of an International Institute for the Unification of Private Law, for which the Italian Government undertook to pay a yearly contribution. The initiative was an application of the system of the League of Nations that provided in Article 24 of the Covenant of the League that:

> There shall be placed under the direction of the League all international bureaux already established by general treaties if the parties to such treaties consent. All such international bureaux and all commissions for the regulation of matters of international interest hereafter constituted shall be placed under the direction of the League.

1. More commonly known by its French acronym OHADA (*Organisation pour l 'harmonisation en Afrique du droit des affaires*).
2. For a general overview of the beginnings of the organization, *see* M. Pilotti, 'Activity of the International Institute for the Unification of Private Law (1926–1946)', *Unification of Law* (Rome: UNIDROIT, 1948): 15 et seq.

In all matters of international interest which are regulated by general Conventions but which are not placed under the control of international bureaux or commissions, the Secretariat of the League shall, subject to the consent of the Council and, if desired, by the parties, collect and distribute all relevant information and shall render any other assistance which may be necessary or desirable.

The Council may include as part of the expenses of the Secretariat the expenses of any bureau or commission which is placed under the direction of the League.

3. While the bureaux included the International Office for Information and Research concerning Assistance to Foreigners (Paris), the International Commission for Air Navigation (Paris), and the Nansen International Office for Refugees (Geneva), specialized institutes were created and linked closely to the League. These included the International Institute of Intellectual Co-operation (Paris), the International Educational Cinematographic Institute (Rome), and subsequently also UNIDROIT.[3]

4. On 30 September 1924, the Assembly decided that the powers and functions of the new Institute, as well as the constitution of its Directing Council (later to become the Governing Council), should be determined by the Council of the League in agreement with the Italian Government. On 3 October 1924, the Council of the League, in conformity with that decision, accepted the offer of the Italian Government.

5. By a letter dated 31 March 1926, the Italian Government confirmed its undertaking to establish and maintain an Institute for the purpose of 'harmonizing and coordinating the rules of Private Law of the different States or groups of States, with a view to promoting gradually the adoption of a uniform system of Private Law by the various States'. This undertaking was to last for a period of seven years, after which it would remain in force for subsequent periods of seven years each unless the Italian Government or the League of Nations should give notice of their intention to terminate its operation at least two years before the expiry of each period. On 20 April 1926, the President of the Council of the League of Nations in turn gave notice of the acceptance by the League of Nations of the offer of the Italian Government.

6. The Institute was consequently founded in 1926 and officially inaugurated on 30 May 1928. The Italian Government placed the Palazzo Aldobrandini in Rome, owned by the State, at the disposal of the Institute. The Italian Government also undertook to build and set up a library with space for 200,000 volumes.

7. Under its Statute of 1926, the Institute was closely connected with the League of Nations. This close link was, however, no longer possible when the Italian Government decided to leave the League. In 1937, the Italian Government, therefore,

3. *See* League of Nations, *Handbook of International Organisations* (1931).

gave the two years notice required by the Statute for the termination of the 1926 agreement. The Italian Government, however, declared that the Institute would continue to exist as an autonomous organization. The League of Nations acknowledged that the Library would remain the property of the Institute.

8. In 1939, the Directing Council then in office (constituted by Messrs. Asquini, Bagge, Basdevant, Graham Harrison, Hennebicq, Kosters, and Manzanilla, under the chairmanship of Mr d'Amelio), aware of the great usefulness of continuing the work already undertaken by the Institute, proposed to the Italian Government that the Institute be reorganized as a Union of States, the Governments of which should give their formal acceptance of the new Statute of the Institute. To that effect, the Directing Council prepared a draft of the new Statute, the text of which was approved by the Council at a meeting held in Florence in May 1939.

9. Italian Government accepted this proposal and invited States, both members of the League of Nations and other Governments, to express their agreement in principle to the new Statute of the Institute. A sufficient number of acceptances having been received, the Italian Government solicited their official participation. The number of adhering Governments contemplated under Article 21 of the Statute, dated 15 March 1940, was not only reached but even surpassed, and the Statute came into force on 21 April 1940.

Part II. Institutional Framework

Chapter 1. The Statute

10. The purpose of UNIDROIT has remained essentially the same as when it was first founded, even if the emphasis and the ways by which the purpose of the organization is achieved have changed with the times. Thus, Article 1 of the 1940 Statute, which albeit slightly modified over the years remains in force, states that the purpose of the organization is to 'examine ways of harmonizing and coordinating the private law of States and of groups of States, and to prepare gradually for the adoption by the various States of uniform rules of private law'.

11. 'Uniform law' is the name given to the regulations adopted in the form of international conventions, protocols, or model laws by States cooperating to find common solutions to specific problems. When they deal with private law, these solutions will affect the lives and activities of individual persons and companies.

12. Ultimately the purposes of the unification of law are to facilitate relations between States and between individuals and businesses of different States by providing for the same, or for a very similar, regulation of those areas of law where relations are most frequent or where the difficulties associated with those relations are such that some form of agreement is imperative, and to promote economic development by the adoption of uniform rules facilitating foreign investments and other relations such as the transfer of technology.

13. Although the origins of uniform law may be traced to the *ius commune*, it was the end of the nineteenth and beginning of the twentieth centuries that saw the first, real development of uniform law. The value of uniform law continued, and continues, to be perceived and appreciated as is clear from its continuing and growing importance in the twentieth century and beyond.

14. The perception of the increasing need for uniform law was aptly summarized by René David when he stated that it is imperative that the task of creating uniform law should be undertaken because of:

> the unprecedented development in our time of international intercourse. Ease of transport, increased mobility of people and capital, international distribution of labour, have resulted in an unprecedented expansion of international commerce. […] Such links mean that complete state independence in matter of

> law results in anarchy: international relations require an international law construed in the same way by the various states concerned. To regulate this intercourse we must find a means of reconstructing a body of law acceptable to all nations […] and we must ensure that the most diverse countries will recognize the value of a body of law destined to govern international relations but which does not emanate from national authority.[4]

15. As indicated above, the current Statute dates to 1940, even if it has been amended over the years. It is quite brief, comprising a mere twenty-two articles, and is integrated by the Regulations of the Institute which provide greater details on internal organization and procedure. Reference to the appropriate provision of the Statute will be made throughout this contribution.

4. R. David, 'The International Unification of Private Law', Ch. 5 of vol. II of the *International Encyclopedia of Comparative Law* (Tübingen, Paris & New York, 1971), 5. On the unification of law, *see also* J. Kropholler, *Internationales Einheitsrecht* (Tübingen: J.C.B. Mohr (Paul Siebeck), 1975).

Chapter 2. Membership

16. Membership of UNIDROIT is restricted to States acceding to the UNIDROIT statute.[5] Currently, UNIDROIT has sixty-five Member States drawn from the five continents, even if Europe and the Americas for historic reasons are more represented than the others.

5. Article 2(2) of the Statute.

Chapter 3. Structure

17. UNIDROIT has an essentially three-tiered structure, made up of a General Assembly of the Member States,[6] a Governing Council elected by the General Assembly, and a Secretariat.

18. The General Assembly is the ultimate decision-making organ of UNIDROIT: it votes on the institute's budget each year, approves the Work Programme every three years,[7] and elects the Governing Council every five years.[8] It is made up of one representative from each member Government.[9] Fifteen members of the General Assembly are elected to serve on the Finance Committee of the General Assembly, which is responsible for a more in-depth examination of the finances of the Institute and makes recommendations to the General Assembly in Plenary.[10] The operation of the General Assembly is specified in more detail in the Regulations of the Institute.[11]

19. The Governing Council supervises all policy aspects relating to the attaining of the Institute's statutory objectives, and in particular, the Secretariat's carrying out of the Work Programme, the drawing up of which is its responsibility.[12] It is made up of one ex officio member, the President[13] of the Institute, who is appointed by the Italian Government,[14] and twenty-five elected members, typically eminent judges, academics and civil servants.[15] A peculiarity of the Governing Council is that although its members are put up for election by their respective countries (sometimes by more States submitting a candidature jointly), the members do not

---

6. Argentina, Australia, Austria, Belgium, Bolivia, Brazil, Bulgaria, Canada, Chile, China, Colombia, Croatia, Cuba, Cyprus, Czech Republic, Denmark, Egypt, Estonia, Finland, France, Germany, Greece, Holy See, Hungary, India, Indonesia, Iran, Iraq, Ireland, Israel, Italy, Japan, Latvia, Lithuania, Luxembourg, Malta, Mexico, Mongolia, Netherlands, Nicaragua, Nigeria, Norway, Pakistan, Paraguay, Poland, Portugal, Republic of Korea, Romania, Russian Federation, San Marino, Saudi Arabia, Serbia and Montenegro,, Singapore, Slovakia, Slovenia, South Africa, Spain, Sweden, Switzerland, Tunisia, Turkey, United Kingdom, United States of America, Uruguay, Venezuela.
7. Article 5(3) of the Statute.
8. Article 6(3) of the Statute.
9. Article 5(1) of the Statute.
10. *See* Art. 16(3) of the Statute and Art. 9 of the Regulations.
11. *See* Arts 1–9.
12. Article 11(2) of the Statute.
13. Mr Vittorio Scialoja (1928–1933).
    Mr Mariano d'Amelio (1934–1943).
    Mr Massimo Pilotti (1944–1959).
    Mr Ernesto Eula (1959–1975).
    Mr Mario Matteucci (1975–1984).
    Mr Riccardo Monaco (1985–1994).
    Mr Luigi Ferrari Bravo (1995–1999).
    Mr Berardino Libonati (2000–2010).
    Mr Alberto Mazzoni (2011-2019).
    Ms Maria Chiara Malaguti (2020).
14. Article 6(2) of the Statute.
15. Article 6(1) of the Statute.

represent their Governments. They sit in a personal capacity, *quae* experts in the law and as the eminent lawyers they are. Over the years, the members of the Council have included eminent personalities such as Ernst Rabel (Germany, 1928–1933), René David (France, 1962–1978), and Ferenc Mádl (1988–2003), who was to become President of the Hungarian Republic in 2000. The Governing Council also examines the budget of the Institute and thereafter makes recommendations to the financial organs of the Institute.[16] The members of the Governing Council are normally closely involved in the work of the Institute, one member of the Council generally chairs the Study Groups set up by the organization.[17] The Regulations of the Institute regulate the Governing Council and its operation in greater detail.[18]

20. The Secretariat is the executive organ of UNIDROIT responsible for the day-to-day carrying out of its Work Programme. It is headed by a Secretary-General,[19] who is appointed by the Governing Council on nomination by the President of the Institute.[20] The Secretary-General is assisted by a staff of international civil servants and various ancillary staff.[21]

16. Article 11(4) of the Statute.
17. Article 13(2) of the Statute.
18. *See* Arts 13–17.
19. Mr Pietro De Francisci (1928–1932).
    Mr Giuseppe Righetti (1934–1937).
    Mr Mario Matteucci(1945–1975).
    Mr Riccardo Monaco(1975–1985).
    Mr Malcolm Evans (1985–1997).
    Mr Walter Rodinò, *ad interim* (1997–1998).
    Mr Herbert Kronke (1998–2008).
    Mr José Angelo Estrella Faria (2008–2017).
    Ms Anna Veneziano, *ad interim* (2017–2018).
    Mr Ignacio Tirado (2018).
20. Article 8(1) of the Statute.
21. *See* Arts 18–22 of the Regulations of the Institute.

Chapter 4. Legal Status

21. Article 2 of the Statute states that the Institute 'shall enjoy, in the territory of each participating Government, the necessary legal capacity to enable it to exercise its functions and to realize its purposes',[22] and that '[t]he privileges and immunities which the Institute and its agents and officers shall enjoy shall be defined in agreements to be concluded with participating Governments'.[23] In application of the latter provision, a Headquarters Agreement was concluded between UNIDROIT and Italy as its host State. This Agreement dates to 1967 and contains provisions for the privileges and immunities that apply to the organization and its staff.[24] Thus, the Agreement contains provisions relating to the seat of the organization,[25] the property of the organization,[26] fiscal facilitations,[27] financial and currency facilitations,[28] privileges and immunities of representatives of Governments and of the organization,[29] and privileges and immunities of the officials of the Institute.[30] The last two of these provisions include the habitual immunity from jurisdiction for acts done in the exercise of their functions and, for the officials of the Institute, within the limits of their functions, including words and writing.[31] Representatives of Governments and of the organization are furthermore exempted from restrictive measures relating to immigration and other formalities to which foreigners are subject.[32] The Agreement was partially revised in 1995, mainly as regards the fiscal facilitations, accorded to the Institute.[33]

22. Article 2(3).
23. Article 2(4).
24. Agreement of 20 Jul. 1967, approved and implemented by Law 1074 of 12 Dec. 1969: *Legge 12 dicembre 1969, n. 1074 Approvazione ed esecuzione dell'Accordo tra il Governo italiano e l'Istituto internazionale per l'unificazione del diritto privato sui privilegi e le immunità dell'Istituto, concluso a Roma il 20 luglio 1967.*
25. Article 1.
26. Article 2.
27. Article 3.
28. Article 4.
29. Article 6.
30. Article 7.
31. Articles 6(1)(a) and 7(1)(a).
32. Article 6(1)(b).
33. Law 193 of 16 Jun. 1997: *Legge 16 giugno 1997,* n. 193 *Ratifica ed esecuzione dello scambio di note costituente un accordo tra il Governo della Repubblica italiana e l'Istituto internazionale per l'unificazione del diritto privato (UNIDROIT) per l'aggiornamento dell'accordo di sede del 20 luglio 1967, fatto a Roma il 5–9 giugno 1995.*

Chapter 5. Languages

22. While UNIDROIT has five official languages (English, French, German, Italian, and Spanish),[34] its working languages are two, English and French. This means that its official publications are issued in two languages and, where possible, work in Study Groups and Committees is also carried out in two languages. There are, however, exceptions: depending on the subject matter dealt with, and also on the financial resources available, work may be conducted in one language only, normally English. The final product is, however, issued in both English and French.

34. Article 10 of the Statute.

Chapter 6. Working Methods

23. UNIDROIT's statutory objective is to prepare uniform rules of private law understood in a broad sense. It is in effect the only organization the activity of which is not limited to any specific area. Thus, alongside commercial law subjects, it deals also with other matters such as cultural property and the law of transport, and in the past, it also dealt with subjects such as intellectual property. The uniform rules prepared by UNIDROIT are concerned with the unification of substantive private law. Normally it does not deal with public law or conflicts of laws, even if the instruments adopted by UNIDROIT will often have a section devoted to issues belonging to these areas of law, in particular, conflicts of laws.

24. In the preparation of its instruments, UNIDROIT avails itself of the assistance of experts in the field, of the collaboration of other international organizations, both intergovernmental and non-governmental, as well as of its network of correspondents. These correspondents are appointed by the Governing Council and are from both member and non-Member States. They assist the Secretariat by providing or retrieving the information needed on the law and legal developments in their countries in the area of interest of any given project. Often experts who have participated in the work of the Study or Working Groups are appointed correspondents and continue to collaborate with the Institute well beyond the conclusion of the work of the Group they were once members of.

§1. TRACING A PROJECT: THE PROCEDURE ADOPTED

I. Preliminary Stage

25. Subjects are normally proposed to the organization by Governments,[35] members of the Governing Council, international institutions or organizations,[36] correspondents and other interested persons who have come across a problem which they feel might suitably be solved by the adoption of an instrument at international level. Every three years, the Secretariat circulates a document containing proposals to Governments, members of the Governing Council, and correspondents. The comments made by those contacted will be submitted together with the proposals to the Governing Council for discussion. If the Council considers a particular proposal to be of interest, it will request a preliminary comparative law study to be prepared. Such a comparative law study will be conducted either by a member of the Secretariat, or by an outside expert. The comparative law study will examine the problem area, the solutions adopted in different jurisdictions, the need for an international instrument, and the feasibility of preparing one. This comparative study will be circulated to interested circles and professional associations for comment.

35. Article 12(1) of the Statute.
36. Article 12(2) of the Statute.

26. The comparative law study and any comments thereon will be submitted to the Council. The Council will decide whether there are good prospects for a viable instrument to be prepared. If so, it will authorize the President of the Institute to convene a Study Group, or Working Group,[37] to examine the problem in greater depth and, if it so decides, to prepare a first draft of a future instrument.

II. Study Groups and Working Groups

27. The members of Study Groups and Working Groups are experts in their field and sit in a personal capacity, as experts and not as representatives of their countries of origin. They are nominated by the President of the Institute on suggestion by members of the Council and the Secretariat. Governments may also be contacted with a request to suggest an expert, it being clearly understood that as members of the Study Group, the experts do not represent their Governments. In the selection of the experts to serve on the groups, a conscious effort is made to ensure the representation of different legal systems, different personal backgrounds so that each expert can contribute with his or her experience, different geographical origin, so that developing countries and countries in transition are adequately represented, and different working languages to ensure that the instrument adopted will be translatable into the different languages of the world. Study Groups are normally quite small, with a maximum of about fifteen members, and, depending on the subject matter dealt with, may have observers from other organizations and from representative international professional associations.

28. Once the Study Group has prepared a draft to its satisfaction, and this includes an assessment of the most suitable type of instrument to be adopted, the draft, at this stage called a 'preliminary draft', will be submitted to the Governing Council. If the Governing Council is satisfied with the product,[38] it will authorize the convening of a Committee of Governmental Experts.[39] It should be noted that this is the procedure followed for international conventions, protocols to conventions and model laws. In the case of other instruments, such as principles or guides, the examination of the final product of the Study or Working Group by the Council will end with the authorization by the Council to publish the instrument.

III. Intergovernmental Negotiation Stage: The Committees of Governmental Experts

29. Full participation in UNIDROIT Committees of Governmental Experts is open to representatives of all UNIDROIT Member States. Non-Member States may be invited to participate as observers. Observers may also include representatives of

37. Article 13(1) of the Statute.
38. Article 14(1) of the Statute.
39. *See* Art. 14(2) of the Statute.

other intergovernmental organizations, non-governmental organizations, and representative international professional associations, for example, the world association of the national professional associations of the area examined. Purely national professional associations are not admitted: they are represented by the worldwide association. Observers may participate in the discussions but are not permitted to vote should a vote be taken.

30. Once the Committee of Governmental Experts has completed its task, the draft instrument as modified by the Committee is submitted to the Governing Council.[40] If the instrument is a draft convention or protocol, the Governing Council will authorize the transmittal of the draft to a Diplomatic Conference[41] that will be convened by one of the Member States of the organization. If the instrument is a model law, the Governing Council will generally endorse the work of the Committee and authorize the publication of the model law.

§2. Choosing the Subject Matter

31. Not all subjects can be dealt with at international level, and not all subjects that can, can be dealt with in the same way. As indicated above, the first point to determine is whether the problems encountered are of a nature that will permit them to be solved by an international instrument. Some purely domestic problems are best dealt with only at domestic level; others, even if they do have international aspects, may be particularly difficult to deal with at international level: family law, which by nature has close links to national, local community, or religious, law, is a case in point.

32. Traditionally, therefore, subjects that have been chosen for international regulation have been subjects that relate almost exclusively to the international sphere and only rarely cross the border into the domestic sphere.

§3. Choosing the Most Appropriate Instrument

33. The choice of instrument must naturally be suitable for the subject matter dealt with. The choice of instrument will, therefore, depend on what is to be regulated.

34. The different instruments that may be adopted have different addressees. International conventions, protocols, and model laws are clearly addressed to legislators. Principles are in the first instance addressed to the parties, arbitrators and judges, even if legislators will often take inspiration from them when they draft legislation. Legislative guides are also addressed to legislators, even if they are not

40. *See* Art. 14(3) of the Statute.
41. *See* Art. 14(4) and (5) of the Statute.

intended to be binding instruments but only to assist legislators. Legal guides, however, are addressed to the parties to an agreement and their legal advisers.

35. Of the different types of instruments that are possible, international conventions are the most rigid. The intention with of an international convention is that it should become part of the national law of the Contracting States more or less as it stands. The possibility to vary the contents of conventions is very limited, as States will only be able to make reservations to specific provisions, and even that may not be possible if the provisions of the convention itself specify that no reservation is possible. How international conventions are incorporated into national legislation will vary from country to country, as will the position of international conventions in the hierarchy of laws. The main advantage of stringent instruments such as international conventions is the fact that they provide for as much legal certainty as is reasonably possible precisely because the texts adopted are incorporated into the legislation of the Contracting States essentially without modification. The other face of the medal is that States may consider certain modifications to be imperative and that as Contracting States, they would not be able to make these changes to the text. The result may be that instead of ratifying or acceding to the convention, they take inspiration from it, just as if it were a model law, and introduce the changes they need. International conventions, because of their characteristics, tend to be opted for when the relations to be regulated are international or cross-border relations.

36. Model laws are more flexible than international conventions. In this case, the intention is from the beginning to permit States to make the changes they consider to be necessary to cater to the specific needs of the country. A further advantage is that it is possible to include in a model law a number of provisions that the experts preparing the law deem to constitute the most appropriate solution to a specific problem, even if some States may want to modify the suggested provision when they take inspiration from it for their national legislation. Whether or not a State does modify a model law, and the extent to which it does so, will depend on the reasons for which it has decided to introduce legislation. The price to pay for this greater flexibility is of course less uniformity, as a number of provisions will differ from country to country. The underlying principles should, however, remain the same. It is these characteristics of the model law that make it more suitable and more used when the instrument to be adopted is to affect domestic conditions.

Chapter 7. Funding

37. After a considerable number of years during which contributions to UNIDROIT were voluntary, and at times even made in kind, mostly in the form of publications for the growing Library, in the 1970s, a system similar to that of the United Nations was adopted. Consequently, its budget is financed by annual contributions from its Member States that are fixed by the General Assembly.[42] For this purpose, States are classified into categories based on the categories of the Contributions Chart of the United Nations.

38. With the general financial crisis of the world, States are able to provide international organizations with only limited funding. In order to come to terms with the increasing financial difficulties of the organization, in 1996, the Governing Council decided to set up a Foundation, the Foundation for the support of UNIDROIT (the UNIDROIT Foundation, formerly the Uniform Law Foundation), for the purpose of retrieving funding for projects and activities that the Institute considered meritorious but which it was not able to fund.[43] After a number of years in which the Foundation was inactive, in 2003 it was felt that the time had come to make the Foundation operative. Professor Sir Roy Goode, a former member of the Governing Council and a collaborator of the Institute for many years, was elected President of the Foundation by the Board of Governors in 2004. He held office until 2013 when he retired and Mr Jeffrey Wool of Freshfields Bruckhaus Deringer, Secretary-General of the Aviation Working Group (AWG) and Condon-Falknor Professor of Global Business Law at the University of Washington (USA), took office.

42. Article 16(1) of the Statute.
43. The Statute of the Foundation was signed on 9 Oct. 1996 by its two co-founders, Mr Luigi Ferrari Bravo, President of UNIDROIT, and Mr Arthur Hartkamp, member of the UNIDROIT Governing Council and at the time Advocate-General at the Supreme Court of the Netherlands.

Part III. Activities

Chapter 1. Introduction

39. The activities undertaken by UNIDROIT, in particular, the Studies it conducts leading to the preparation and adoption of international instruments are all given a Study Number, usually indicated by Roman numerals. The numbers are normally in chronological order, although at times when a subject is revisited the number used when the subject matter was first dealt with might be resumed. A complete list of the studies undertaken so far is to be found in Appendix 1 *infra*, whereas a list of the international instruments adopted either by the Institute itself or by other organizations, with which UNIDROIT was cooperating is to be found in Appendix 2. An up-to-date status of ratifications for each of the UNIDROIT Conventions is to be found on the UNIDROIT website, at: <www.unidroit.org>. For a description of the working methods followed at UNIDROIT, *see* Part II, Chapter 6, *supra*.

Chapter 2. International Sale of Goods (Study IV)

40. The unification of the law of international sales is one of the first areas UNIDROIT worked on. It was already in 1929 that, at the proposal of Ernst Rabel, UNIDROIT decided to undertake the necessary preparatory studies and to entrust the preparation of a future uniform law to a Committee presided over by Cecil J.B. Hurst and including eminent comparative lawyers such as E. Rabel himself, A. Bagge, H. Capitant, M. Fehr, H.C. Gutteridge, and J. Hamel.[44] In 1934, the Committee submitted a preliminary draft of an international law on the sale of goods to the Governing Council of UNIDROIT. The Council approved the draft and transmitted it together with an Explanatory Report to the League of Nations in order to solicit comments from Member States. In light of the comments received, the Committee revised the text, and in 1939, the Governing Council adopted a revised version of the draft. Work was interrupted by war. It was, therefore, only in 1951 that the Government of the Netherlands convened a Conference to adopt the text. It was, however, decided that a Special Commission should be appointed to further elaborate the text.[45] Two separate drafts were produced by the Committee, one in 1956, the other in 1963. In the meantime, UNIDROIT produced a separate draft uniform law dealing with the formation of international sales contracts.

41. In view of the favourable reactions to the two draft instruments, the Government of the Netherlands convened a Diplomatic Conference for their final adoption. The Diplomatic Conference was held in The Hague (2–25 April 1964). The two instruments adopted were the Convention relating to a Uniform Law on the International Sale of Goods (ULIS), and the Convention relating to a Uniform Law on the Formation of Contracts for the International Sale of Goods (ULFC). The two instruments entered into force in 1972.

42. Four years after the adoption of the 1964 Hague Conventions, UNCITRAL requested the Secretary-General of the United Nations to transmit to all Member States of the United Nations the text of both ULIS and ULFC to ask for their position vis-à-vis the two instruments and whether they intended to adhere.

43. An analysis of the replies to the questions revealed that the two instruments were considered to be too European in character and were, therefore, not favoured by a majority of States. UNICTRAL consequently began to work on what was to become the 1980 United Nations Convention on Contracts for the International Sale of Goods (CISG), which had a broader basis even if it was prepared on the basis of the 1964 Conventions. With the adoption of the 1980 Convention, the interest of the

44. *See* C.M. Bianca & M.J. Bonell, *Commentary on the International Sales Law: The 1980 Vienna Sales Convention* (Milan: Giuffrè, 1987), 3 et seq. The colon inserted in the footnote is not in the title of the book. Please reinstate the hyphen in the manuscript.
45. *See* Final Act of the Conference on a Draft Convention relative to a Uniform Law on the Sale of Goods held at The Hague, 1–10 Nov. 1951, in *Unification of Law (1947–1952)* (Rome: UNIDROIT, 1954), 283 et seq.

two 1964 instruments became largely historical. To all intents and purposes, the 1980 Convention has replaced the two Hague Conventions.

§1. CONVENTION RELATING TO A UNIFORM LAW ON THE FORMATION OF CONTRACTS FOR THE INTERNATIONAL SALE OF GOODS (ULFC)

44. The Uniform Law on the Formation of Contracts for the International Sale of Goods specifically governs the formation of contracts for the International Sale of Goods. According to Article 1(1):

> [t]he present Law shall apply to the formation of contracts of sale of goods entered into by parties whose places of business are in the territories of different States, in each of the following cases: (a) where the offer or the reply relates to goods which are in the course of carriage or will be carried from the territory of one State to the territory of another; (b) where the acts constituting the offer and the acceptance are effected in the territories of different States; (c) where delivery of the goods is to be made in the territory of a State other than that within whose territory the acts constituting the offer and the acceptance are effected.

According to Article 1(6), however, it shall not 'apply to the formation of contracts of sale: (a) of stocks, shares, investment securities, negotiable instruments, or money; (b) of any ship, vessel or aircraft, which is or will be subject to registration; (c) of electricity; (d) by authority of law or on execution or distress'.

§2. CONVENTION RELATING TO A UNIFORM LAW ON THE INTERNATIONAL SALE OF GOODS (ULIS)

45. The Uniform Law on the International Sale of Goods governs the obligations of the seller and the buyer arising from the contract of sale. It does not govern the formation of the contract, which is covered by ULFC, nor does it deal with the capacity of the parties or with vitiating factors.[46] Furthermore, the Uniform Law is not concerned with the effects that the conclusion of a contract may have on the property of the thing sold, nor is the Uniform Law concerned with the validity of any of its provisions or with the validity of usages on which the parties may rely.

46. According to Article 1(1):

> [t]he present Law shall apply to contracts of sale of goods entered into by parties whose places of business are in the territories of different States, in each of

46. *See* A. Tunc, 'Commentary of the Hague Conventions of 1 Jul. 1964 on the International Sale of Goods and on the Formation of Contracts of Sale' (The Hague: Dutch Ministry of Justice), 18 et seq. Also published in Volume I (Acts) of the Records and Documents of the Diplomatic Conference on the Unification of Law Governing the International Sale of Goods, 2–25 Apr. 1964 (The Hague: Ministry of Justice of the Netherlands, Government Printing Office, 1966), 357 et seq., at 363.

> the following cases: (a) where the contract involves the sale of goods which are at the time of the conclusion of the contract in the course of carriage or will be carried from the territory of one State to the territory of another; (b) where the acts constituting the offer and the acceptance have been effected in the territories of different States; (c) where delivery of the goods is to be made in the territory of a State other than that within whose territory the acts constituting the offer and the acceptance have been effected.

According to Article 5(1), however, it does not apply 'to sales: (a) of stocks, shares, investment securities, negotiable instruments or money; (b) of any ship, vessel or aircraft, which is or will be subject to registration; (c) of electricity; (d) by authority of law or on execution or distress'.

§3. Tripartite Legal Guide to Uniform Legal Instruments in the Area of International Commercial Contracts (with a Focus on Sales) (Study L)

47. In December 2015, the United Nations Commission on International Trade Law (UNCITRAL) invited UNIDROIT and the Hague Conference on Private International Law to cooperate on a project for the creation of a roadmap to the existing texts in the area of international sales law (sales contracts) prepared by each organization, primarily the CISG, the UNIDROIT Principles and the Hague Principles, and providing an assessment of interactions between the texts, their actual and potential use, application and impact, in order to promote their appropriate use, uniform interpretation, and adoption. Such a project should 'extend also, as relevant, to the other texts in the field prepared by the three organizations (including, for example, the Limitation Convention, the Electronic Communications Convention, the 1983 Uniform Rules, ULIS/ULFC 1964, and the 1955/1986 Hague Conventions), and make reference, as needed, to outside instruments (e.g., those of regional economic integration organizations such as the EU, OHADA, as well as those of the ICC, ITC)'.

48. The Governing Council decided to recommend this topic for inclusion by the General Assembly in the UNIDROIT Work Programme for the triennium 2017–2019. The General Assembly endorsed this recommendation at its 75th session, on 1 December 2016.

49. The work was entrusted to a panel of experts on international commercial contract law and/or private international law composed of Professors Neil B. Cohen (Brooklyn Law School, US), Lauro Gama Jr (Pontifícia Universidade Católica do Rio de Janeiro, Brazil), Hiroo Sono (Hokkaido University, Japan), Pilar Perales Viscasillas (Universidad Carlos III de Madrid, Spain), and Stefan Vogenauer (Max Planck Institute for Legal History and Legal Theory, Germany). The outcome is a joint publication and online tool reflecting the contributions of the organizations with legislators, judges, arbitrators, and/or lawyers and commercial operators as target audiences.

50. The Guide was unanimously approved at the 99th session of the UNIDROIT Governing Council (remote session, April/May 2020), subject to such minor amendments that might result from the discussion of the text at the 53rd session of the UNCITRAL Commission scheduled for July 2020. It was approved by the UNCITRAL Commission and published in 2021 by the United Nations in its official languages. It is accessible on the websites of UNCITRAL and UNIDROIT.

Chapter 3. International Commercial Contracts (Study L)

§1. PRINCIPLES OF INTERNATIONAL COMMERCIAL CONTRACTS (STUDY L)

51. Work on what were to become the UNIDROIT Principles of International Commercial Contracts began following a Decision of the Governing Council in 1971 which in the French version spoke of an *essai d'unification portant sur la partie générale des contrats (en vue d'une Codification progressive du droit des obligations 'ex contractu').*[47] The project originally had the title 'Progressive Codification of International Trade Law', but as work progressed, it became clear that what had begun in the intentions of the proponents as a binding codification was better dealt with as a non-binding instrument. The project was, therefore, renamed Principles of International Commercial Contracts.

52. A special Working Group was set up in 1980. After a slow start due to prior commitments, work took on momentum in 1986, the first part being completed, and publication authorized by the Governing Council in 1994. A second, enlarged edition was published in 2004, a third edition again enlarged was finalized in 2010 and published in 2011 and the fourth edition, which specifically takes into account the requirement of long-term contracts was finalized and approved by the Governing Council in 2016 and published in 2017.

53. The Principles constitute a system of rules of contract law specifically adapted to the special requirements of modern commercial practice which may in a number of important ways be of service to the international community. They may in particular be chosen by the parties as the law governing their contract or referred to by arbitrators in the settlement of disputes; they may be used as a means of interpreting or supplementing existing international uniform law instruments such as the 1980 United Nations Convention on Contracts for the International Sale of Goods and may also serve as a model for international legislators when drafting new legal instruments or for national lawmakers when adapting domestic law to meet modern requirements.[48]

54. The 1994 Principles consisted of a preamble and 119 articles divided into seven chapters (General Provisions, Formation, Validity, Interpretation, Content, Performance, and Non-Performance). The Chapter on Performance contains a special section on Hardship, while the Chapter on Non-Performance deals with such questions as the Right to Performance, Termination, and Damages. Each article is accompanied by detailed comments, including illustrations, which form an integral part of the Principles.

55. When deciding in 1994, the publication and widest possible distribution of the UNIDROIT Principles, the Governing Council stressed the need 'to monitor their

47. *See* document U.D.P. 1971, Conseil de direction, 50ème session, Rome, 26–29 avril 1971, Procès-verbaux, 93.
48. *See* the Preamble to the Principles.

use with a view to a possible reconsideration of them at some time in the future'. At its 75th session, held in 1996, the Governing Council was seized of a report by the Secretariat containing first proposals as to future work on the UNIDROIT Principles. Following this report, the Governing Council requested the Secretariat to submit to the 1997 Council session, one or more papers suggesting areas not dealt with in the first part of the Principles that could be included in a second part and, possibly, indicating problem areas that might have been identified in relation to the 1994 text.

56. At its 76th session in April 1997, the Governing Council was seized of the results of a questionnaire sent out to practitioners which reflected the success of the Principles in actual practice and decided that work be resumed with priority with a view to the preparation of a second part and that to this end a new Working Group be set up.

57. The Working Group decided to give priority to the following topics: agency, limitation of actions (extinctive prescription), assignment of contractual rights and duties, contracts for the benefit of a third party, set-off, and waiver. In addition, certain modifications were introduced into the 2004 text to adapt it to electronic contracting. The Working Group completed its work in 2003 and the Governing Council approved the Principles of International Commercial Contracts 2004 at its session in May 2004.

58. When it adopted the second edition of the Principles, the Governing Council recommended that, in view of their success worldwide, the Principles should figure in the Institute's Work Programme as an ongoing project. Consequently, in 2005, the Council instructed the Secretariat to set up a new Working Group to prepare a third edition. The new Working Group, the core members of which remained the same, started work in 2006. The last meeting of the Working Group was held in 2010, and the third edition of the Principles was published in 2011 after a last review by the Governing Council that same year.

59. In the third edition, Chapter 3 was divided into sections, the existing provisions being divided into Section 1 (General Provisions) and Section 2 (Defects of Consent). Article 3.17(1) became Article 3.2.14, Article 3.17(2) became Article 3.2.15, and Article 3.19 was moved and became Article 3.1.4. A new Section 3 (Illegality) was added. A new Section 3 (Conditions) was added to Chapter 5, and the Article on Restitution in Chapter 7 (Article 7.3.6) was replaced by two articles: Article 7.3.6 on Restitution with respect to contracts to be performed at one time and Article 7.3.7 on Restitution with respect to contracts to be performed over a period of time. A new Chapter 11 was added on the Plurality of Obligors and of Obligees.

60. In 2013, the Governing Council was seized of a document that examined the possibility of again taking up work on the Principles, with the intention of addressing long-term contracts within the context of the Principles, which it was felt, had not been adequately covered in the present Principles. The General Assembly endorsed this recommendation.

61. In 2015, a Working Group for the preparation of the fourth edition of the Principles was set up. It held two sessions, approving modifications, mainly to the comments to take the requirements of long-term contracts into consideration. Only six provisions were amended, i.e., the Preamble and Articles 1.11, 2.1.14, 5.1.7, 5.1.8, and 7.3.7. The alterations made to the Comments were in particular made to the Comments on the Preamble (amendments to Comment 2) and Articles 1.11 (addition of a new Comment 3), 2.1.14 (amendments to Comments 1–3 and addition of a new Comment 4), 2.1.15 (amendments to Comment 2 and addition of a new Comment 3), 4.3 (amendments to Comment 3 (which has become Comment 4) and addition of a new Comment 3), 4.8 (amendments to Comments 1–3), 5.1.3 (amendments to the Comment (which has become Comment 1) and addition of a new Comment 2), 5.1.4 (addition of a new Comment 3), 5.1.7 (amendments to Comments 2–3), 5.1.8 (amendments to the Comment (which has become Comment 1) and addition of a new Comment 2), 7.1.7 (addition of a new Comment 5), 7.3.5 (amendments to Comment 3 and addition of a new Comment 4), 7.3.6 (amendments to Comment 1), and 7.3.7 (amendments to Comments 1–2).[49]

62. The Governing Council approved the modifications at its 75th session in May 2016. The fourth edition was published in May 2017.

63. The UNIDROIT Principles 2016 thus consist of:

- The Preamble;
- Chapter 1: General Provisions;
- Chapter 2: Formation and Authority of Agents:
  - Section 1: Formation;
  - Section 2: Authority of Agents;
- Chapter 3: Validity:
  - Section 1: General Provisions;
  - Section 2: Grounds for avoidance;
  - Section 3: Illegality;
- Chapter 4: Interpretation;
- Chapter 5: Content and Third-Party Rights:
  - Section 1: Content;
  - Section 2: Third-Party Rights;
  - Section 3: Conditions;
- Chapter 6: Performance:
  - Section 1: Performance in General;
  - Section 2: Hardship;
- Chapter 7: Non-Performance:
  - Section 1: Non-Performance in General;
  - Section 2: Right to Performance;
  - Section 3: Termination;

49. *See* UNIDROIT Principles of International Commercial Contracts 2016, Introduction to the 2016 Edition, p. vii.

  - Section 4: Damages;
- Chapter 8: Set-off;
- Chapter 9: Assignment of Rights, Transfer of Obligations, Assignment of Contracts:
  - Section 1: Assignment of Rights;
  - Section 2: Transfer of Obligations;
  - Section 3: Assignment of Contracts;
- Chapter 10: Limitation Periods;
- Chapter 11: Plurality of Obligors and of Obligees:
  - Section 1: Plurality of obligors;
  - Section 2: Plurality of obliges.

The total number of articles is now 211.

64. A database devoted to the CISG and the UNIDROIT Principles (the UNILEX database), which includes bibliographical references but also, most importantly, case law decided on these two instruments, was set up by the Centre for Comparative and Foreign Law Studies, a research centre set up jointly by UNIDROIT, the University of Rome I '*La Sapienza*' and the Italian National Research Council. In the case of the Principles, most decisions are arbitral awards, for which reason it is not possible to include the full text of the decision but merely case summaries, which however are of the greatest interest in evaluating the Principles and their importance. The database is available online at: <www.unilex.info>.

§2. MODEL CLAUSES FOR THE USE OF THE UNIDROIT PRINCIPLES OF INTERNATIONAL COMMERCIAL CONTRACTS (STUDY L)

65. Despite the success of the Principles, there is a clear perception that the potentialities of the Principles in transnational contract and dispute resolution practice have not yet been fully realized, largely due to the fact that the Principles are still not sufficiently well-known in the international business and legal communities. The idea was, therefore, launched that Model Clauses be prepared, that the parties might adopt in order to indicate in what way they wished the UNIDROIT Principles to be used during the performance of the contract or when a dispute arose. The Model Clauses reflect the different ways in which the UNIDROIT Principles are in practice referred to by parties or applied by judges and arbitrators.

66. The four different ways in which the Model Clauses can be used and incorporated into the contract of the parties are:

(1) to choose the Principles as the rules of law governing the contract;
(2) to incorporate the Principles as terms of the contract;
(3) to refer to the Principles to interpret and supplement the CISG when the latter is chosen by the parties; or

(4) to refer to the Principles to interpret and supplement the applicable domestic law, including any international uniform law instrument incorporated into that law.

67. Clearly, in deciding which of the four categories of Model Clauses to choose, parties should be aware of the advantages and disadvantages of each and to help the parties' comments and remarks accompany the text. Where appropriate, each category of Model Clause proposes two versions, one for inclusion in the contract ('pre-dispute use') and one for use after a dispute has arisen ('post-dispute use').

68. The *Model Clauses for Use by the Parties of the UNIDROIT Principles of International Commercial Contracts* were adopted by the Governing Council of UNIDROIT at its 92nd session in May 2013 and published that same year.

§3. FORMULATION OF PRINCIPLES OF REINSURANCE CONTRACTS (STUDY L)

69. In July 2015, UNIDROIT was approached by a group of scholars and practising lawyers led by Professor Anton K. Schnyder and Professor Helmut Heiss (University of Zurich), Professor Martin Schauer (University of Vienna) and Professor Manfred Wandt (University of Frankfurt), who were examining the feasibility of formulating 'Principles of Reinsurance Contract Law' (PRICL). This initiative was inspired by the project group 'Restatement of European Insurance Contract Law', which had led to the publication of the Principles of European Insurance Contract Law (PEICL).[50] The purpose of the project is to formulate a 'restatement' of existing global reinsurance law, which is largely embedded in international custom and usage but is seldom the object of legislation. The project leaders observed that the proposed principles presupposed the existence of adequate rules of general contract law. They stated that rather than attempt to re-create such rules, the proposed new principles should be drafted as a 'special part' of the UNIDROIT Principles of International Commercial Contracts.

70. In addition to the project managers, the research team includes well-known representatives from Belgium, Brazil, China, Germany, France, Great Britain, Italy, Japan, Singapore, South Africa, and the United States. In addition, two advisory groups with representatives of the global insurance and reinsurance markets advise the research team. The intention is to draft specific principles and comments on: choice-of-law, non-disclosure, errors and omissions, conditions precedent, event/accumulation/aggregation, late notice, back-to-back cover, 'follow the fortunes' and 'follow the settlement' principles, cooperation, time bar rule, termination and recapture, and extra-contractual obligations of the reinsured.

50. Principles of European Insurance Contract Law, Edited by Project Group 'Restatement of European Insurance Contract Law', established by Fritz Reichert-Facilides†, Chairman: Helmut Heiss, Sellier European Law Publishers (October 2009).

71. The Governing Council decided to recommend this topic for inclusion by the General Assembly in the UNIDROIT Work Programme for the triennium 2017–2019. The General Assembly endorsed this recommendation of the Governing Council at its 75th session on 1 December 2016.

72. At its 98th session (2019), the Governing Council took note of the finalized version of the black-letter rules and comments of the PRICL and authorized the Secretariat to link to the text of the PRICL from the UNIDROIT Website once the publication was finalized. The Principles of Reinsurance Contract Law (PRICL) are thus available on the website of the University of Zurich and linked from that of UNIDROIT.

73. On 22 December 2018, the Secretariat was informed that the Working Group had received funding from the Swiss National Science Foundation and the German Research Foundation to support the project for another triennium (1 July 2019–30 June 2022). The topics to be addressed in that triennium are: 'Chapter VI: Back-to-Back-Cover; Chapter VII: Non-contractual Liability Clauses; Chapter VIII: Termination and Recapture; Chapter IX: Limitation Periods'. Due to the connections between a number of these topics and the UNIDROIT Principles of International Commercial Contracts, the PRICL Working Group asked UNIDROIT to continue its involvement under the same conditions as before (i.e., in-kind contribution through participation of a representative in the biannual Working Group meetings). This proposal was approved by the UNIDROIT Governing Council at its 98th session and recommended for adoption by the General Assembly. The General Assembly endorsed the continuation of the project for the 2020–2022 Work Programme at its 2019 session. It was however not possible to bring the project to completion within this timeframe as a result of the suspension of the in-person activity of the Working Group during the pandemic period. The extension of the project for one, possibly two, years so as to bring it to a conclusion in 2024 was approved by the General Assembly at its 81st session in December 2022.

Chapter 4. Agency (Study XIX)

74. The Convention on Agency in the International Sale of Goods was adopted in Geneva in 1983. As is explained in the Explanatory Report to the Convention, the Convention should not be viewed as an attempt to codify the law relating to international agencies:

> rather it should be seen as a supplement, albeit an important one, to the existing conventions dealing with the international sale of goods, namely the 1964 Hague Conventions, which themselves originated as UNIDROIT drafts, relating to Uniform Laws on the International Sale of Goods and on the Formation of Contracts for the International Sale of Goods and, more recently, the United Nations Convention on Contracts for the International Sale of Goods […].[51]

The reason for this is that:

> those conventions […] do not deal with certain special aspects of contracts for the international sale of goods concluded through an agent and the fact that the Vienna Convention itself is the fruit of some 50 years work, first in UNIDROIT and then in UNCITRAL, is a testimony to the difficulties which had to be overcome in the elaboration of the Geneva Convention, since unification in the field of agency is considerably more difficult to achieve than in relation to contracts of sale. This is so not only because the agency relationship is of a tripartite character but also on account of the distinctions made in the various legal systems with regard to the buying and selling of goods through agents.[52]

75. As indicated in the Explanatory Report, the:

> main aim of the Convention is to establish as simple and clear a regime as possible to govern the legal consequences of the acts of an agent who has been authorised by a principal to conclude a contract of sale of goods with a third party and to this end it has been framed in such a way as to regulate virtually all situations which are common in international trade.[53]

The Convention does not deal with the internal relations between the principal and the agent, although a number of years later, it was proposed that work on these relations be undertaken. Interest in also covering the internal relations however waned with the adoption of the European Community Agency Directive and work was therefore abandoned.

51. M. Evans, 'Convention on Agency in the International Sale of Goods: Explanatory Report', *Uniform Law Review* (1984): 81, para. 11.
52. *Ibid.*
53. M. Evans, 'Convention on Agency in the International Sale of Goods: Explanatory Report', *Uniform Law Review* (1984): 85, para. 16.

76. The Agency Convention has not to date entered into force, although it has served as a source of inspiration for other drafts, such as what was to become the section on Agency in the Principles of International Commercial Contracts.

Chapter 5. Leasing (Study LIX)

§1. The 1988 Unidroit Convention on International Financial Leasing

77. In May 1988, a Diplomatic Conference convened by the Canadian Government and held in Ottawa saw the adoption of two Unidroit conventions: the Unidroit Convention on International Financial Leasing and the Unidroit Convention on International Factoring. The two conventions were opened for signature on 28 May 1988.

78. The scope of application of the Convention on International Financial Leasing was consciously limited to what is known as 'financial leasing', the intention being to prepare a separate legal infrastructure to remove the existing legal uncertainty which hampered the realization of the full potential of financial leasing at cross-border level.

79. Two factors were considered by the authors of the convention as of crucial importance in distinguishing the financial lease from neighbouring legal concepts to which it had almost invariably been assimilated. The first of these factors was the:

> dynamic, pivotal role played in the transaction by the lessee who selects the equipment and supplier on its own with a concomitant reduction in the role of the lessor whose ownership is stripped of virtually all the normal attributes of that quality and whose interest in the transaction is the purely financial one of recouping its capital investment; secondly, the leasing agreement between lessor and lessee is concluded for a term which takes the period of economic amortisation of the equipment into consideration, whence the essentially financial nature of the transaction for the lessor, in that the lessee's payment of its rentals is not merely consideration for its rights to use of the equipment, as would be the case with a typical bailment, but also guarantees the lessor the amortisation of its capital investment.[54]

80. As is explained in the Explanatory Report to the Draft Convention, it was felt that the restriction of the scope of application of the draft Convention to the tripartite financial lease was essential to the draft's whole underlying philosophy:

> in that the reason for insulating the lessor in most cases from liability for the condition of the equipment was because its role was purely financial in character, a consideration which would not apply in the typical operating lease, particularly in that type of operating lease where the lessor produces the equipment itself. Likewise, one of the principal reasons for focussing on financial leasing was precisely to deal with those special legal problems that arise

54. Explanatory Report on the Draft Convention on International Financial Leasing prepared by the Unidroit Secretariat (Study LIX – Doc. 48), published in *Diplomatic Conference for the Adoption of the Draft Unidroit Conventions on International Factoring and International Financial Leasing – Acts and Proceedings, Vol. I* (Rome, 1991), 39, para. 32.

out of the complex, tripartite nature of financial leasing, in particular the absence of contractual nexus between the supplier and the lessee, problems which do not arise with the typical bipartite operating lease. There was not the same need for an international instrument, indeed for any legislation at all, where all the parties had to do was to write their own contract, as was the case with the typical bipartite operating lease.[55]

81. Originally the intention had been to cover financial leasing in general, but the reluctance of certain States to adopt international instruments that affect their domestic law determined that the Convention's application was limited to international financial leasing, although it was recognized that, as a majority of States had no domestic legislation which specifically addressed financial leases, the convention might in any event, serve as a source of inspiration for national legislators intending to adopt domestic legislation.[56]

82. The provisions of the Convention are divided into three parts: a first part with articles that delimit the Convention's sphere of application, both substantive and geographic, and also includes general provisions (Chapter I, Articles 1–6), a second part forming the main body of substantive uniform rules which deal with the rights and duties of the parties (Chapter II, Articles 7–14), and a third with the final provisions (Chapter III, Articles 15–25).

§2. THE MODEL LAW ON LEASING (STUDY LIX A)

83. At its 78th session (1998), the Governing Council decided to include the preparation of a model law on leasing in the Institute's Work Programme, drawing on the expertise already gained by UNIDROIT in this field, with a view to formulating a coherent response to the requirements of those developing countries and countries in economic transition engaged in the reform of their domestic leasing laws. Other commitments of the organization, notably those relating to the preparation of the convention and related protocols on International Interests in Mobile Equipment, postponed work on this project.

84. Work, however, did start in October 2005, and was conducted first by a Study Group and then by a Committee of Governmental Experts. The Model Law was adopted in November 2008 by a Joint Session of the UNIDROIT General Assembly and the Committee of Governmental Experts. The Explanatory Report illustrating the Model Law was prepared by the UNIDROIT Secretariat in 2010, as instructed by the Joint Session. The Model Law is limited to commercial leases and does not govern consumer leases, and covers only leases of assets that are 'used in the craft, trade or business of the lessee'.[57]

55. *Ibid.*, 41, para. 36.
56. *Ibid.*, 41, para. 38.
57. Article 2, Definition of 'asset'.

Chapter 6. Factoring (Study LVIII)

85. The Diplomatic Conference that saw the adoption of the UNIDROIT Convention on International Financial Leasing also adopted the UNIDROIT Convention on International Factoring.

§1. THE 1988 UNIDROIT CONVENTION ON INTERNATIONAL FACTORING (STUDY LVIII)

86. The decision to prepare uniform rules for international factoring was based on the recognition that trade would be encouraged by facilitating factoring. It was also agreed both by the Study Group and the Committee of Governmental Experts that unification should be limited to international factoring, considering that such a restriction would be conducive to the acceptance of the uniform rules by a greater number of States, as:

> while it might be desirable in theory to contemplate the preparation of uniform rules on factoring at national level as well as international level, there could well be a strong reluctance on the part of many States to accept changes to well-established principles of law which are of much more general application than simply to factoring transactions. While the committee opted, as regards the form of the future instrument, in favour of a Convention, it emphasized on a number of occasions in the course of its work that this choice would leave it open to those States which wished to do so to draw on the international rules when preparing national legislation directed to domestic transactions.[58]

87. As the Explanatory Report on the draft explains:

> the Committee decided to limit the scope of its work of unification to what may be considered the keystone of factoring transactions, namely the specific question of assignments, and to lay down basic minimum principles concerning a restricted number of aspects raising particular problems. Furthermore, it should be pointed out that the rules governing the mechanics of assignments are limited to the relationship between the three parties directly interested – the assignor, the assignee and the debtor – to the exclusion of situations involving third parties […]. As regards on the other hand the problems relating to priorities between the rights of the factor and those of third parties in the receivables, it is on account of their extreme complexity that the committee decided not to deal with them, by way of a substantive rule of law or of a conflicts rule,

58. Explanatory Report on the Draft Convention on International Factoring prepared by the UNIDROIT Secretariat (Study LVIII – Doc. 33), published in *Diplomatic Conference for the Adoption of the Draft UNIDROIT Conventions on International Factoring and International Financial Leasing – Acts and Proceedings Vol. I* (Rome, 1991), 88, para. 10.

and this notwithstanding the widely expressed regret that the Convention failed to regulate an aspect of the question which created very great difficulties at international level.[59]

88. The Convention is divided into four parts: the first covering the sphere of application and general provisions (Chapter I, Articles 1–4), the second dealing with the rights and duties of the parties (Chapter II, Articles 5–10), the third with subsequent assignments (Chapter III, Articles 11–12) and the fourth containing the final provisions (Chapter IV, Articles 13–23).

§2. Factoring Model Law (Study LVIIIA)

89. As indicated in §1 above, the Unidroit Convention on International Factoring is limited to international factoring, although international factoring represents only 21% of global factoring, with domestic factoring accounting for 79%. Despite the importance of domestic factoring, no intergovernmental organization has as yet adopted a factoring model law to assist States in undertaking reforms to improve their domestic legal framework.

90. In December 2018, the World Bank proposed that Unidroit include the preparation of a model law on factoring in its 2020–2022 Work Programme. The proposal noted that existing instruments largely focused on international or cross-border transactions and did not provide sufficient guidance to States to develop functional domestic factoring frameworks. At its 98th session in May 2019, the Unidroit Governing Council approved the insertion of the project into the 2020–2022 Work Programme as a high-priority project. The General Assembly endorsed this recommendation by the Council at its 78th session (2019). A Working Group was therefore set up and started operation in July 2020.

91. The purpose of the future Model Law is to provide an instrument for States that want to introduce a new factoring law or to update their existing laws but are not in a position to undertake a comprehensive secured transactions law reform. It will consist of black-letter rules accompanied by a limited commentary on each rule to explain its operation. The preparation of the Model Law takes UNCITRAL's work in this field into especial consideration, in particular, the United Nations Convention on the Assignment of Receivables in International Trade (2001), the UNCITRAL Legislative Guide on Secured Transactions (2007) and the UNCITRAL Model Law on Secured Transactions (2016). The pandemic having delayed work also on this project, the General Assembly at its December 2022 session endorsed the recommendation of the Governing Council to retain the preparation of a Model Law on Factoring as a high-priority project in the Institute's 2023–2025 Work Programme, in order to allow both the finalization and adoption of the Model Law and the preparation of a Guide to Enactment for the Model Law.

59. *Ibid.*, para. 10. Add the 88 before para.10.

Chapter 7. International Interests in Mobile Equipment (Study LXXII)

92. In June 1988, the Canadian Government proposed that UNIDROIT launch an effort designed to extend the principle of a lessor's real rights being enforceable against its lessee's trustee in bankruptcy and unsecured creditors, enshrined in the UNIDROIT Convention on International Financial Leasing, to the field of security rights in mobile equipment in general. The proposal was based on the consideration that the cost of credit for high-value mobile equipment was exceedingly high because, under the conflict of laws rule of the applicability of the *lex rei sitae*, the creditor's position was uncertain.

§1. THE 2001 CAPE TOWN CONVENTION ON INTERNATIONAL INTERESTS IN MOBILE CONVENTION (STUDY LXXII)

93. In November 2001, a Diplomatic Conference was convened in Cape Town by the Government of South Africa and sponsored jointly by the ICAO and UNIDROIT to adopt a Convention on International Interests in Mobile Equipment as well as the first of three equipment-specific Protocols, namely the Protocol on Matters Specific to Aircraft Equipment. The Convention and Protocol were opened for signature on 16 November 2001.

94. In the words of the Chairman of the Drafting Committee and author of the Official Commentary, Sir Roy Goode, the:

> Convention is designed to establish an international legal regime for the creation, enforcement, registration and priority of security interests and interests held by chargees, conditional sellers and lessors in three categories of high-value, uniquely identifiable mobile equipment, namely (a) airframes, aircraft engines and helicopters […] (b) railway rolling stock, and (c) space assets. The Convention is not itself equipment-specific and for each of the three categories of object it applies only through separate Protocols.[60]

In other words, the Convention applies to any category of equipment covered by a protocol only as among the States party to that protocol, and subject to the terms of the protocol.

95. As the Official Commentary further elaborates, the:

> principal objective of the Convention is to facilitate the efficient financing and leasing of mobile equipment. Such financing will assist in the development of cost-effective modes of transport and space assets utilising modern

60. *See* the Introduction to R. Goode, *Convention on International Interests in Mobile Equipment and Protocol Thereto on Matters Specific to Aircraft Equipment – Official Commentary*, 1st ed. (Rome, 2002), 2, para. 3.

technologies. The Convention system is designed to bring significant economic benefits to countries at all stages of economic development, and in particular to developing countries by bringing within their reach commercial finance for mobile equipment that has previously been unavailable or available only at relatively high cost. A sound, internationally adopted legal regime for security, title-retention and leasing interests will encourage the provision of finance and leasing and reduce its cost.[61]

96. The Official Commentary identifies five key objectives for the Convention and Protocols:

(1) To facilitate the acquisition and financing of economically important items of mobile equipment by providing for the creation of an international interest which will be recognized in all Contracting States.
(2) To provide the creditor with a range of basic default and insolvency-related remedies and, where there is evidence of default, a means of obtaining speedy relief pending final determination of its claim on the merits.
(3) To establish an electronic international registry for the registration of international interests which will give notice of their existence to third parties and enable the creditor to preserve its priority against subsequently registered interests and against unregistered interests and creditors in the debtor's insolvency.
(4) To ensure through the relevant Protocol that the particular needs of the industry sector concerned are met.
(5) By these means to give intending creditors greater confidence in the decision to grant credit, enhance the credit rating of equipment receivables and reduce borrowing costs to the advantage of all interested parties.[62]

97. The following paragraph, however, stresses the Conventions and Protocols:

'have very specific objectives and do not seek to cover the whole field of asset-based secured financing, much of which will continue to be governed by national laws and the agreement of the parties'.[63] The Convention itself allows considerable scope for party agreement on a range of issues, including default remedies and jurisdiction.[64]

§2. The 2001 Cape Town Protocol on Matters Specific to Aircraft Equipment (Study LXXII D)

98. The Aircraft Protocol was the first of the equipment-specific Protocols to be adopted. Indeed, it was adopted together with the base Convention and was opened

61. *Ibid.*, 3rd ed. (Rome, 2013), 13, para. 2.1.
62. *Ibid.*, 3rd ed. (Rome, 2013), 15, para. 2.6.
63. *Ibid.*, 3rd ed. (Rome, 2013), 17, para. 2.(3).
64. *Ibid.*, 3rd ed. (Rome, 2013), 18, para. 2.9(4).

for signature the same day. It is intended to meet the particular needs of aircraft financing. Two basic objectives were identified by the authors of the Protocol:

> First, the Convention/Aircraft Protocol must facilitate the asset-based financing and leasing of aircraft equipment, increasing the availability and/or reducing the cost of aviation credit. [...] Secondly, the final instrument must generate a high level of international consensus, particularly among the States with significant objective interests in the sale and financing of aircraft equipment. [...].[65]

99. As indicated above, the Convention and each of the Protocols operate together with respect to the equipment specifically dealt with in the Protocols. In the case of the Aircraft Equipment Protocol, the Convention and Protocol apply to airframes, aircraft engines, and helicopters, collectively termed 'aircraft objects'.[66] Article III of the Protocol extends the scope of the Convention to cover also outright sales and prospective sales of aircraft objects to the extent that the provisions are relevant to such sales. The Aircraft Equipment Protocol was prepared by an Aircraft Protocol Group (APG), set up at the invitation of the President of UNIDROIT. The core membership of the APG included representatives of the ICAO, the International Air Transport Association (IATA), and the AWG.

100. The Aircraft Protocol and the Convention as applied to aircraft objects entered into force on 1 March 2006, following the deposit of the eighth instrument of ratification/accession. The International Registry became operational on 1 March 2006 when the Convention and Aircraft Protocol entered into force. It is accessible online at: <www.aviareto.aero/>.

§3. THE 2007 LUXEMBOURG PROTOCOL ON MATTERS SPECIFIC TO RAILWAY ROLLING STOCK (STUDY LXXII H)

101. Each Protocol must clearly cater to the needs of the industry concerned. In the case of railway rolling stock, the situation is different from that of the aircraft industry. Whereas there are only a handful of commercial aircraft manufacturers in an industry dominated by two giants, in the rail sector, there are over a hundred manufacturing companies in Europe alone.[67] The first draft of the Rail Protocol was prepared by Mr Howard Rosen, coordinator of the Rail Working Group (RWG), for

65. *See* J. Wool, 'The Case for a Commercial Orientation to the Proposed UNIDROIT Convention as Applied to Aircraft Equipment', in *A New International Regimen Governing the Taking of Security in High-Value Mobile Assets: The Legal and Economic Implications*, a special issue of the *Uniform Law Review* (1999): 289 et seq., at 291.
66. *See* Art. 2(3)(a) of the Convention.
67. H. Rosen, 'Creating an International Security Structure for Railway Rolling Stock: An Idea Ahead of Its Time?', in *A New International Regimen Governing the Taking of Security in High-Value Mobile Assets: the Legal and Economic Implications*, a special issue of the *Uniform Law Review* (1999): 313, at 318.

consideration by the RWG in Plenary. At the intergovernmental stage, UNIDROIT collaborated with the Intergovernmental Organisation for International Carriage by Rail (OTIF).[68]

102. There is a growing realization of the importance of railways:

> [t]he rail system offers environmentally acceptable means of transportation of goods and people at a time when distribution is ever more important and at a time when the other means of distribution (particularly by road and air) are becoming increasingly overloaded.[69]

The decision to prepare a Protocol for railway rolling stock was, *inter alia,* derived from considerations that in many jurisdictions:

> there is no watertight security system since in the past, State funding of railways has rendered it unnecessary. Moreover, often rolling stock can migrate, temporarily or permanently, across borders. As a result, even if security can be perfected in a specific jurisdiction, the financier remains exposed if the asset moves across a border.[70]

Clearly, the situation raises considerable difficulties for the privatization of railways as a result of the need of States to reduce their involvement.

103. The Protocol applies to railway rolling stock and according to Article I(2)(e) of the Rail Protocol:

> 'railway rolling stock' means vehicles movable on a fixed railway track or directly on, above or below a guideway, together with traction systems, engines, brakes, axles, bogies, pantographs, accessories and other components, equipment and parts, in each case installed on or incorporated in the vehicles, and together with all data, manuals and records relating thereto.

104. The draft Protocol was adopted on 23 February 2007 by a diplomatic Conference held in Luxembourg. It has not yet entered into force, and preparations are underway for the establishing of the International Registry (*see* below).

105. A Preparatory Commission for the establishment of an International Registry under the Luxembourg Protocol was set up by Resolution No. 1 of the Luxembourg Diplomatic Conference. Eleven sessions, convened jointly by UNIDROIT and the Intergovernmental Organisation for International Carriage by Rail (OTIF),

68. *Organisation intergouvernementale pour les transports internationaux ferroviaires.*
69. H. Rosen, 'Creating an International Security Structure for Railway Rolling Stock: An Idea Ahead of Its Time?', in *A New International Regimen Governing the Taking of Security in High-Value Mobile Assets: the Legal and Economic Implications*, a special issue of the *Uniform Law Review* (1999): 313, at 314.
70. *Ibid.*, at 315.

have been held to date (March 2023). The 6th Session of the Preparatory Commission was held to approve the draft contracts, their annexed schedules and related documents (software security agreement; deed of business continuity) for the establishment and operation of the International Registry for railway rolling stock. The 7th Session (11 December 2014) took note of the signature of the contract between the Preparatory Commission and Regulis SA. and discussed and approved the draft baseline Regulations for the International Registry for railway rolling stock. The 8th session (6–7 December 2018) approved the Statutes and the Rules of Procedure of the Supervisory Authority. The 9th session (8 April 2021) approved a revised version of the Draft Regulations for the International Registry to be issued in due course by the Supervisory Authority. The Commission was also briefed on developments since the last Preparatory Commission session and on the activities of the Ratification Task Force, which are aimed at reaching the number of adhesions required for the entry into force of the Protocol and the operability of the international Registry. It was also informed of the activity of the Group of Experts established by UNECE for the Permanent Identification of Railway Rolling Stock (PIRRS). The 10th session (August 2021, by e-mail) was convened to confer a mandate upon a Negotiating Team with a view to the change in ownership and control of the Registry-designate Regulis SA, the possibility of which had been brought to the attention of the Preparatory Commission Co-Chairs in 2020, and any related necessary adjustments of the contracts for the operation of the International Registry. The 11th session (Rome and remote, 29–30 November 2022) approved the proposed change of control in the Registry-designate Regulis S.A. from the International Communications and Technology Group SITA (SITA BV) to Information Services Corporation (ISC) Atlantic Services Inc. It also approved the proposed amendments to the 2014 Agreements for the operation of the Registry and the assignment of the Master Service Agreement, the Software Security Agreement and the Deed of Business Continuity from SITA Ireland to ERS.

§4. The 2012 Berlin Protocol on Matters Specific to Space Assets (Study LXXII J)

106. The Protocol on Matters specific to Space Assets was prepared by the Space Working Group (SWG), a body composed of representatives of the worldwide aerospace industry, satellite operators, and the financing community, as well as representatives of the United Nations Office for Outer Space Affairs (UNOOSA), the European Space Agency/European Centre for Space Law and the IBA. It was set up in 1997 for the purpose of promoting the space industry's interests as connected with the future Convention, as well as to prepare the Protocol.

107. Space assets as defined by the Protocol are:

> any man-made uniquely identifiable asset [capable of being independently owned, used or controlled,] in space or designed to be launched into space, and comprising

(i) a spacecraft, such as a satellite, space station, space module, space capsule, space vehicle or reusable launch vehicle, whether or not including a space asset falling within (ii) or (iii) below;
(ii) a payload (whether telecommunications, navigation, observation, scientific or otherwise) in respect of which a separate registration may be effected in accordance with the regulations; or
(iii) a part of a spacecraft or payload such as a transponder, in respect of which a separate registration may be effected in accordance with the regulations,

together with all installed, incorporated or attached accessories, parts and equipment and all data, manuals and records relating thereto.[71]

Where 'space' means outer space, including the Moon and other celestial bodies' (Article I(2)j).

108. The nature of space assets is very different from other types of equipment, in particular, as regards jurisdictional questions. For example:

> many legal systems do not adequately provide for the registration and perfection of security interests in space property. In those jurisdictions that recognize non-possessory pledges of personal property and that have debtor-based systems of recording security interests, such as jurisdictions whose legal systems derive from British common law, a security interest in an orbiting satellite can be created in the same manner as ordinary earth-based collateral.[72]

109. In addition to these difficulties, which are not new:

> the nature of satellite financing has changed markedly in the last decade, thereby increasing the necessity for an appropriate legal regimen. In particular, a new type of financing customer has gained prevalence. Previously, commercial satellites were owned and transponders were leased almost exclusively by governmental agencies and well-capitalized, blue chip companies. […] More and more frequently, however, satellite owners and lessors are start-up companies with limited capital, unproven credit-standing and little history of operating success. Often the satellite or the transponder and its associated rights, such as contractual and licensing rights, are the only significant assets of the company. Consequently, the ability to take a valid, perfected security interest in these assets may determine whether or not a satellite project can be successfully implemented.[73]

71. Article I(2)(k).
72. D.A. Panahy & R. Mittal, 'The Prospective UNIDROIT Convention on International Interests in Mobile Equipment as Applied to Space Property', in *A New International Regimen Governing the Taking of Security in High-Value Mobile Assets: the Legal and Economic Implications*, a special issue of the *Uniform Law Review* (1999): 303, at 305.
73. *Ibid.*

110. At the intergovernmental stage, work continued with the assistance of the SWG and also with the collaboration of the other organizations involved (UNOOSA, the European Space Agency/European Centre for Space Law and the IBA). The draft Protocol was adopted on 9 March 2012 by a Diplomatic Conference held in Berlin (27 February–9 March 2012). It has not yet entered into force, and preparations are underway for the establishing of the International Registry (*see* below).

111. Pursuant to Resolution No.1 of the Berlin Diplomatic Conference, a Preparatory Commission was set up to act under the guidance of the UNIDROIT General Assembly as Provisional Supervisory Authority for the establishment of the International Registry for Space Assets. At the 1st session of the Preparatory Commission (6 and 7 May 2013), eleven States agreed to serve as members and, in addition, a number of other participants and representatives of the financial and commercial world attended as observers. In particular, the International Telecommunication Union (ITU) accepted to join the Commission and confirmed its interest in considering it becoming the Supervisory Authority, subject to the conditions set forth in Resolution No. 2 of the Final Act of the Berlin Diplomatic Conference. The Preparatory Commission appointed two Working Groups, one entrusted with the development of rules for the International Registry for Space Assets and the other with the drafting of a request for proposals for the selection of a Registrar. The Commission invited Sir Roy Goode to produce, with the assistance of the Secretariat of UNIDROIT and on the basis of comments received by the members of the Preparatory Commission, a first draft of the Registry Regulations accompanied by an Explanatory Memorandum clearly indicating the open points where input from industry and other experts would be most needed.

112. At its 2nd session (27–28 February 2014), the Preparatory Commission considered the revised draft of the Registry Regulations and the accompanying explanatory report prepared by Sir Roy Goode. At the outcome of the session, an agreement in principle was reached on most of the provisions of the draft Registry Regulations, whilst the remaining open questions were the object of a further revised document by Sir Roy Goode circulated for comments in May 2014 (in particular the post-launch criteria to identify satellites where no serial number is available as well as the identifiability of separate parts of a space asset such as transponders). During the 2nd session of the Preparatory Commission, the representatives of ITU reaffirmed the interest of their organization in accepting the role of Supervisory Authority for the future Registry for space assets. They informed the Preparatory Commission of the forthcoming ITU meetings during which the question would be discussed (the ITU Council meeting (May–June) and the meeting of the Conference of Plenipotentiaries (October–November)).

113. At its 3rd session (11 and 12 September 2014), the Preparatory Commission finalized the text of the Regulations with the exception of the issue of the identification criteria for parts of spacecraft, for which a consultation procedure on an agreed draft text was suggested in order to receive further insights from the practical operators in the market. Finally, the ITU representative reported on the positive outcome of the ITU Council meeting in May 2014 and reiterated the interest of ITU to be considered the natural candidate for the role of Supervisory Authority. At its 4th session (10 and 11 December 2015), the Commission finalized the text of the Registry Regulations and also addressed issues concerning the selection of a Registrar and the appointment of a Supervisory Authority. The 5th session of the Preparatory Commission (6 December 2017) was convened to discuss the progress in the selection of the Registrar, and the appointment of a Supervisory Authority, as well as future promotional events.

§5. The Pretoria Protocol on Matters Specific to Agricultural, Mining, and Construction Equipment (MAC Protocol) (Study LXXII K)

114. In the course of the preparation of the three Protocols originally planned, a couple of Member States expressed interest in the preparation of an additional Protocol on matters specific to agricultural equipment. To agricultural equipment mining and construction equipment were added by the Governing Council at its 85th session in 2006.

115. The preliminary investigation went through a number of stages: a questionnaire eliciting the view of Member States but also of non-Member States that had been involved in the Cape Town process, on the utility of a fourth Protocol was circulated in 2006, the replies being submitted to the Governing Council at its 86th session in 2007; a tentative draft Protocol first submitted to the Council at its 87th session in 2008 was circulated among the States contacted in 2008, their comments and suggestions being submitted to the Council at its 88th session in 2009. At that session, the Council asked the Secretariat to seek ways of narrowing down the scope of the proposed Protocol by again contacting States and interested private circles.

116. Thus, as indicated above, between 2005 and 2012, a range of background research activities were conducted in relation to the project, including consultations with private industry and a preliminary economic analysis.

117. A Study Group, which was composed of various international experts, met four times between 2014 and 2016 to consider legal issues associated with the preparation of the MAC Protocol and to prepare a preliminary draft text. In addition to the members of the Study Group, the meetings were attended by observers from various international organizations and academic institutions.

118. At its 95th session (2016), the Governing Council considered the draft text produced by the Study Group and decided that it was sufficiently developed to warrant the convening of a Committee of Governmental Experts.

119. The Committee of Governmental Experts met twice, in March and October 2017 respectively. The most hotly debated issues were: (i) the scope of the Protocol in relation to MAC equipment; (ii) how the Protocol should address interests arising out of the association of MAC equipment with immovable property; and (iii) the amendment procedure for the Protocol, with particular regard to the Harmonized System codes (HS codes) contained in the Annexes to the preliminary draft Protocol.

120. The draft finalized by the Committee of Governmental Experts was submitted to the Governing Council at its 97th session. The Council decided that it was ripe for adoption and consequently authorized the convening of a Diplomatic Conference. The Protocol was finally adopted by a Diplomatic Conference convened by South Africa and held in Pretoria on 11–22 November 2019.

121. Pursuant to Resolution 1 of the Diplomatic Conference, a Preparatory Commission was established to act as Provisional Supervisory Authority until the entry into force of the Protocol. The Preparatory Commission operates under the guidance of the Governing Council and General Assembly of UNIDROIT. The three key responsibilities of the Preparatory Commission are: (1) the selection of a Registrar to operate the MAC Protocol International Registry; (2) the establishment of a Supervisory Authority; and (3) the preparation of the first edition of the International Registry Regulations.

122. The first session of the Preparatory Commission was held on 21–22 May 2020. At that session, the Preparatory Commission adopted its Rules of Procedure and considered several issues associated with the future operation of the International Registry. The Commission also established a Working Group to draft a request for proposals for the selection of a Registrar (the Registrar Working Group), as well as a Working Group to develop draft Regulations for the International Registry (the Regulations Working Group). Finally, the Commission extended the period available to the International Finance Corporation (IFC) to accept the role of Supervisory Authority. The second session of the Preparatory Commission took place on 10–11 December 2020, the third session took place on 3 and 4 June 2021 to consider matters relating to the appointment of a Supervisory Authority, updates on the activities of the Regulations Working Group and updates on the activities of the Registrar Working Group. The fourth session of the Preparatory Commission took place on 17 and 18 January 2022 and again considered matters relating to the appointment of a Supervisory Authority, updates on the activities of the Regulations Working Group and updates on the activities of the Registrar Working Group. The fifth session of the Preparatory Commission took place on 22 and 23 November 2022 and considered the Report of the Evaluation Committee and selection of a Registrar, matters relating to the appointment of a Supervisory Authority, updates on the activities of the Regulations Working Group, update on the implementation and establishment of a Ratification Task Force and the 2022 revision of the Harmonized System

Chapter 8. Secured Transactions in General (Study LXXII A)

123. At its 72nd session (1993), the Governing Council, in response to a reference from the Study Group for the Preparation of Uniform Rules on Certain International Aspects of Security Interests in Mobile Equipment, decided to include the subject of Secured Transactions in General in the Work Programme of the Institute. The intended purpose of this project is to study the desirability and feasibility of the preparation of a model law in the general field of secured transactions.

124. Although preliminary work was carried out by a Restricted Working Group, the members and chairman of which were co-opted from the Sub-Committee responsible for the preparation of a first draft of uniform rules on certain international aspects of security interests in mobile equipment, priority was accorded to the pursuance of work on the Institute's international interests in mobile equipment project.

Chapter 9. Franchising (Study LXVIII)

125. UNIDROIT's work on franchising saw two distinct stages, each stage with its own distinct product as the outcome: Stage One produced the Guide to International Master Franchise Arrangements published in 1998 (second edition 2007) and Stage Two the Model Franchise Disclosure Law which was adopted in 2002.

126. Franchising was first drawn to the attention of UNIDROIT in 1985 when the then-Canadian member of the Governing Council of the organization proposed that the Institute should consider drafting uniform rules for franchising. In those years, UNIDROIT was engaged in the preparation of what were to become the UNIDROIT Conventions on International Financial Leasing and International Factoring, and the Council member saw the preparation of uniform rules on franchising as a natural development in the process of the preparation of uniform rules for the new types of agreement that were emerging at the time. Furthermore, there had been instances of sharp practices which it was feared might be exported with franchising, which was beginning to spread across the world as a form of business.

127. An initial opposition to the project, in particular among franchisors, as well as prior commitments of the Institute, put the project on hold until 1993 when it was decided that the time had come to set up a Study Group. Opposition was still strong, but a consensus was reached on the utility of a Guide to master franchising, which was recognized as the form of franchising most important for international franchising. It was further decided to postpone a final decision as regards the utility of adopting legislation specifically for franchising at the international level.

§1. THE GUIDE TO INTERNATIONAL MASTER FRANCHISE ARRANGEMENTS

128. Work on the Guide started immediately following the acceptance of the recommendations of the Study Group by the Governing Council and was brought to fruition in a very short period of time: in February 1998, the Governing Council of UNIDROIT authorized the publication of the UNIDROIT Guide to International Master Franchise Arrangements, which appeared in September 1998. The French version of the Guide, under the title '*Guide sur les accords internationaux de franchise principale*', was published in 2000 and the Spanish version ('*Guía de UNIDROIT para los Acuerdos de Franquicia Principal Internacional'*) was published exclusively online in 2005. A second edition of the English version of the Guide, incorporating the novelties that had occurred since 1998 as regards national and international legislation, was published in 2007.

129. What the Study Group felt to be of particular importance when it wrote the Guide, was to ensure that a lawyer using the Guide would be able to find the information he or she needs to obtain the best possible deal when negotiating an agreement, or, considering other possible users, that a judge or arbitrator would have sufficient information to understand the intricacies of the arrangement when deciding a case, or that a legislator would be able to have the information he or she needs when drafting legislation. In addition, the Guide might be used to train young lawyers, and therefore be inserted in the course materials, as has indeed been proposed.

§2. The Model Franchise Disclosure Law

130. At the same session as it authorized, the publication of the Guide to International Master Franchise Arrangements, the Governing Council of the Institute accepted a proposal by the Secretariat of the organization that the Study Group on Franchising should proceed with the preparation of a model law.

131. The submission of the Secretariat was based on the growing interest demonstrated by the franchising community. This growth of interest was largely due to the increasing attention devoted to franchising by legislators and the consequent proliferation of franchise laws. The franchising community felt that the legislation that had been adopted in a number of countries demonstrated a certain lack of understanding of franchising and risked severely hampering its development. Consequently, they felt that the adoption of similar legislation in other countries should if possible be avoided. If UNIDROIT prepared a model law, which by definition would be a balanced instrument considering the nature of the organization and the guarantees offered by its past history, this would make available to legislators an instrument that would promote and not hamper the development of franchising.

132. As regards the subject matter to be dealt with, the Study Group observed that one of the characteristics of franchising was that a large number of areas of law were involved, a majority of which had already been regulated. It would be extremely difficult to justify adopting a regulation specifically for franchising in relation to, for example, contract law, choice of law and jurisdiction, or intellectual and industrial property law. However, one aspect of the franchise relationship that was essential to all types of franchising was the need for disclosure. Furthermore, disclosure was not extensively regulated and it made sense to adopt specific regulations for disclosure in franchising. It was, therefore, decided that the subject matter that should be dealt with was disclosure.

133. Considering that the provisions on disclosure should apply to both domestic and international franchising, it was decided that the type of instrument that should be adopted was a model law.

134. The Model Law was finally adopted by the Governing Council of the Institute in 2002. The Model Law is intended to serve as a model to those legislators that have decided to adopt franchise-specific legislation and is intended to apply to franchising irrespective of its origin, domestic or international. It is further designed to cover different types of franchise agreements, such as traditional unit agreements, master franchise agreements, and development agreements.[74]

74. *See* the Explanatory Report on the Model Franchise Disclosure Law for a history of the development of the project, as well as for an explanation of each of the provisions of the Model Law.

Chapter 10. Transactions on Transnational and Connected Capital Markets (Study LXXVIII)

135. At its 80th session (2001), the Governing Council of UNIDROIT decided to include a project on Transactions on Transnational and Connected Capital Markets in the Work Programme of the Institute. Five topics were included in the project:

(1) the creation of clear and consistent rules for the taking of securities, especially securities held indirectly through intermediaries in multi-tier holding patterns and evidenced by book entries in the investor's account, as collateral;
(2) the creation of standardized 'global shares' permitting trade of such shares on more than one (national) stock exchange so as to make foreign capital markets accessible to a wider range of companies with limited means to create genuinely global shares on a case-by-case basis;
(3) the development of rules capable of enhancing trading on emerging markets;
(4) the development of harmonized or uniform substantive rules applicable to so-called 'delocalized' transactions – such delocalization may be the consequence of mergers between markets located in different jurisdictions or it may be technologically induced where 'Electronic Communications Networks' (ECNs) are used for trading and even initial public offerings of securities; and
(5) the examination of the desirability and feasibility of rules for worldwide takeover bids.

136. In view of budgetary restrictions, the project is being conducted on an item-by-item basis.

§1. THE 2009 GENEVA CONVENTION ON SUBSTANTIVE RULES FOR INTERMEDIATED SECURITIES

137. The challenge the Study Group faced in the preparation of 'Harmonized substantive rules regarding securities held with an intermediary' was to draft an international instrument capable of improving the worldwide legal framework for securities' holding and transfer, with special emphasis on cross-border situations. A Position Paper prepared by the Study Group outlined the Group's views on the scope of the future instrument.

138. While important progress was made by the EU Directives on Financial Collateral Arrangements (2002) and Settlement Finality in Payment and Securities Settlement Systems (1998), aimed at harmonizing key aspects of the laws of EU Member States relevant to securities settlement systems and indirectly held securities, as well as by the Hague Convention on the Law Applicable to Certain Rights in respect of Securities held with an Intermediary adopted in 2002 which addresses concerns relating to conflict of laws issues, these instruments do not cover the full spectrum of concerns identified: EU Directives operate only at the regional level, and while it is hoped that the Hague Convention will in due course extend worldwide, it is by its nature confined to conflict of laws issues.

139. The issues at stake can be divided into the two categories of internal soundness, which comprises issues relating to the key features which any structure for the holding and transfer of securities through intermediaries must possess if it is to be regarded as sound, bearing in mind, in particular, the objectives of investor protection and efficiency, and compatibility, which comprises issues affecting the ability of different legal systems to connect successfully where securities are held or transferred across national borders.

140. On 9 October 2009, the UNIDROIT Convention on Substantive Rules for Intermediated Securities was finally adopted in Geneva, the Diplomatic Conference having been held in two parts, both in Geneva. The first part was held from 1 to 12 September 2008, the second from 5 to 9 October 2009. The provisions included in the Convention treat questions as important as investor protection in case of the insolvency of its securities custodian (bank or broker) and protection of the entire financial system as such against the so-called systemic risk, that is, a chain reaction of financial institutions falling insolvent due to legal uncertainty in the global securities market. The Chapters cover the Rights of the Account Holder (Chapter II), the Transfer of Intermediated Securities (Chapter III), the Integrity of the Intermediated Holding System (Chapter IV), and Special Provisions in Relation to Collateral Transactions (Chapter V). The Official Commentary to the Convention was published by Oxford University Press in 2012.

§2. PRINCIPLES AND RULES CAPABLE OF ENHANCING TRADING IN SECURITIES IN EMERGING MARKETS (UNIDROIT LEGISLATIVE GUIDE ON INTERMEDIATED SECURITIES)

141. It will be recalled that 'the development of rules capable of enhancing trading on emerging markets' was one of the five parts into which the project on Capital Markets was divided (*see* paragraph 135 *supra*). The Governing Council on a number of occasions reiterated the importance it attached to this topic.[75] Consequently, the UNIDROIT General Assembly at its 65th session in 2009 included work on a 'Legislative Guide on principles and rules capable of enhancing trading in securities in emerging markets' in the UNIDROIT Work Programme.[76]

142. The first step in the development of a legislative guide was the preparation of an Accession Kit to the 2008 Intermediated Securities Convention to provide guidance for countries that ratify the Convention on how best to incorporate the Convention and integrate it into their domestic legal systems. An important part of this Accession Kit was advice on the formulation of declarations and models of declarations that may be lodged under the Convention. In addition to offering technical

75. *See*, for example, document UNIDROIT 2009 – C.D.(88) 17, para. 59.
76. *See* document UNIDROIT 2009 – A.G.(65) 10, paras 18 and 26.

advice on the formulation of declarations, the Accession Kit also contains a discussion of, and advice explaining how to address, the issues that the Convention does not address or which it allows Contracting States to provide for otherwise. The work done in the preparation of the Accession Kit by canvassing all the other areas of law that affect or support the development of a modern financial market laid the ground for the work on the broad legislative guide to principles and rules capable of enhancing trading in securities in emerging markets.

143. An informal group of experts assisted the Secretariat with the preparation and review of the provisionally entitled 'UNIDROIT Legislative Guide on Intermediated Securities: Implementing the Principles and Rules of the Geneva Securities Convention'. The informal Group held three meetings (23–24 October 2015, 16–17 May 2016 and 12–13 December 2016), and a follow-up videoconference (16 January 2017) to review the revised draft, which was subsequently circulated again for comments and was submitted to the Committee for review. The Committee held its fourth meeting in Beijing, China (29–30 March 2017), at the kind invitation of the China Securities Regulatory Commission, which hosted it jointly with the China Securities Depository and Clearing Corporation Ltd. The Members and Observers of the Committee, as well as other States and organizations, reviewed in detail the draft Legislative Guide on Intermediated Securities. They agreed upon certain amendments and additions, and ultimately recommended that the draft Legislative Guide, as revised, be submitted to the UNIDROIT Governing Council at its following session. The Governing Council thus considered and adopted the Legislative Guide on Intermediated Securities at its 96th session (Rome, 10–12 May 2017).

144. The Legislative Guide seeks to enhance legal certainty and economic efficiency with respect to the holding and transfer of intermediated securities, in both domestic and cross-border situations, in either of two ways: first, by complementing the Geneva Securities Convention, it is hoped that the Legislative Guide will promote its adoption and implementation, and second, by summarizing the Convention's key principles and rules, it is hoped that, even where the Convention is not adopted, such principles and rules can be chosen and implemented.

§3. NETTING OF FINANCIAL INSTRUMENTS

145. The netting of financial instruments had been mentioned for a number of years as a possible area of work for UNIDROIT. Indeed, in 2008, the Governing Council recommended its inclusion in the Work Programme of the Institute.[77] A consultation of the International Derivatives Association (ISDA) following the crisis of the financial markets in 2008/2009 evinced the opinion that the fundamental assumption of this project had not only not been affected by the crisis, which indeed had made more evident the need for an instrument, the main purpose of close-out netting arrangements and master agreements of this type being to limit the systemic

77. *See* document UNIDROIT 2008 – C.D.(87) 23, 17 et seq.

risk of default and insolvency in financial markets.[78] A full study of the subject was thereupon commissioned by a former collaborator of the Institute and submitted to the Governing Council at its 89th session in 2010.[79] Having examined this study, the Council decided to recommend to the General Assembly that netting be included in the Work Programme of the Institute.[80] The General Assembly, at its 67th session on 1 December 2010, endorsed this recommendation and decided to include netting in the Work Programme of the Institute with high priority.

146. The Principles on the Operation of Close-Out Netting Provisions were adopted by the Governing Council of the Institute at its 92nd session in 2013 and published that same year, the text having been elaborated first, by three sessions of a Study Group, thereafter by two sessions of a Committee of Governmental Experts.

78. *See* document UNIDROIT 2009 – C.D.(88) 17, 5, para. 27.

79. *See* document UNIDROIT 2010 – C.D.(89) 7 Add. 2 'Systemic risk, regulatory powers and insolvency law – The need for an international instrument on the private law framework for netting', by Dr Philipp Paech, Senior Research Fellow Institute for Law and Finance, University of Frankfurt.

80. *See* document UNIDROIT 2010 – C.D.(89) Misc. 4.

Chapter 11. Civil Procedure (Study LXXVI)

§1. ALI/UNIDROIT PRINCIPLES OF TRANSNATIONAL CIVIL PROCEDURE

147. In 1998, the American Law Institute (ALI) proposed to collaborate with UNIDROIT on the preparation of transnational rules of civil procedure. When submitting this proposal to the Governing Council of UNIDROIT (77th Session, February 1998), the then Director of the ALI, Mr Geoffrey Hazard, referred to a preliminary draft which he and Mr Michele Taruffo, Professor of Comparative Civil Procedure in the University of Pavia had prepared and stressed that the project was compatible with the work being carried out by the Hague Conference on Private International Law in the field of international jurisdiction and the recognition and enforcement of foreign judgments in civil and commercial matters. The ALI project dealt with the situation arising once the question of jurisdiction had been settled and before the question of recognition and enforcement of the judgment arose. Moreover, the ALI project concerned only transnational disputes, namely disputes in which the parties were nationals of different States. The basic idea was that whenever this kind of dispute was brought before a court, it would be advisable that the same rules applied regardless of which State court had jurisdiction. This very simple idea was, nevertheless, hard to put into effect not only on account of the differences existing between Common law and Civil law systems but also on account of the differences existing within each system.

148. At its 78th Session (1999), the Governing Council was seized of a feasibility study and, on the basis of the favourable conclusion reached by that study, decided to set up a joint UNIDROIT-ALI Working Group for the Preparation of Transnational Rules of Civil Procedure. The Working Group completed its work in 2003, and the Governing Council of the Institute authorized the publication of the Principles at its session in 2004.

§2. FORMULATION OF REGIONAL RULES: ELI – UNIDROIT MODEL EUROPEAN RULES OF CIVIL PROCEDURE (STUDY LXXVIA)

149. Within the framework of the institutional cooperation with the newly founded European Law Institute (ELI), UNIDROIT and the ELI initiated a joint project for the preparation of European transnational rules of civil procedure which use the ALI/UNIDROIT Principles of Transnational Civil Procedure as a basis for their preparation.

150. Nine Working Groups were established on: access to information and evidence; provisional and protective measures; service of documents and due notice of proceedings; *lis pendens* and res judicata; obligations of parties, lawyers and judges; costs; judgments; parties; and a structure group with the mandate to 'coordinate the emerging draft rules within a functional whole' and to provide 'oversight of linguistic issues'.

151. The Working Groups started work at different times, both to permit some experts to participate in more than one Working Group and to facilitate consideration. The Working Groups were expected to submit their draft rules and comments by 2018 in order to permit a consolidated text to be submitted to the Governing Council in May 2018 and a finalized text to be prepared by early 2019.

152. The schedule was adhered to and the ELI-UNIDROIT Model European Rules of Civil Procedure, accompanied by Comments, were finalized and approved by the ELI Council and Membership in the summer of 2020, as well by the UNIDROIT Governing Council at the second meeting of its 99th session (23–25 September 2020). They were published by Oxford University Press in August 2021 and are also available on the websites of both UNIDROIT and ELI. The French version was finalised in 2022 and is due to be published in 2023.

§3. BEST PRACTICES FOR EFFECTIVE ENFORCEMENT (STUDY LXXVIB)

153. In December 2018, the Secretariat received a proposal from the World Bank for the 2020–2022 Work Programme for the 'Development of a Working Paper to Outline Best Practices on Debt Enforcement'. This proposal was discussed by the Governing Council as a continuation, and a refinement, of the 'Principles of Effective Enforcement' project, which was already on the 2017–2019 Work Programme as part of the Institute's work on civil procedure. The project was included in the 2020–2022 Work Programme by the General Assembly at its 78th session (2019) in endorsement of the recommendation of the Governing Council at its 98th session (2019). The Secretariat was asked to produce a more refined scope of the project to be presented to the Governing Council at its 99th session in 2020. As a result of the difficulties to hold an in-person meeting of the Governing Council in 2020, the 99th session was divided into two, the first part essentially being a consultation by mail (April/May 2020), the second a hybrid in-person/remote session (23–25 September 2020). During the April/May discussions, Council members reviewed the Secretariat document and authorized the setting up of a consultation procedure to receive expert feedback on the questions raised.

154. The UNIDROIT Secretariat consequently developed a Consultation Document including, *inter alia,* a set of questions designed to better define the most appropriate guidance to be given to the future Working Group in determining the type of instrument envisaged and the scope of the project. All participants in the consultation process recognized the fundamental importance of procedures and mechanisms for effective enforcement of creditors' claims, both in transnational situations and in domestic civil proceedings, taking into account the need to ensure the effective legal protection of contractual rights. They also agreed on the existence in most jurisdictions of numerous challenges for enforcement, as well as on the lack of a comprehensive and sufficiently detailed international instrument providing guidance for national legislators to overcome such challenges.

155. Prior to the September meeting of the Governing Council, the Secretariat organized a workshop (21 September 2020) at which input from experts with different backgrounds, international organizations working in the field and members of the UNIDROIT Governing Council, was sought, especially in relation to the determination of the most appropriate guidance to be given a future working group as to the scope of the project and the impact of technology on enforcement. At its September meeting, the Governing Council approved the guidelines prepared by the Secretariat regarding the proposed scope of the project, confirmed the high-priority status assigned to the project, and authorized the establishment of a Working Group. The first meeting of the Working Group, held in Rome and on Zoom 30 November – 2 December 2020, was followed by intersessional work conducted by three informal subgroups, SubGroup 1 on 'post-adjudication' enforcement, Subgroup 2 on the enforcement of secured claims (collateral) and Subgroup 3 on the impact of technology on enforcement. The second meeting of the Working Group was held on 20–22 April 2021 and the third meeting was held from 29 November to 1 December 2021. A general examination of the development of the project was followed by a discussion of issues of the enforcement of monetary claims by third-party debt orders, including tentative best practices regarding the impact of automation; charging orders on land and some aspects of complex enforcement relating to special types of assets; and draft best practices on security rights over receivables, the disposition of collateral and the variation by parties of the rules regarding the realization of the collateral.

Chapter 12. Model Law on Warehouse Receipts (Study LXXXIII)

156. In 2019, the Secretariat of UNCITRAL invited the UNIDROIT Secretariat to consider joint work on warehouse receipts, in particular, the possibility of drafting a Model Law. The reasons for this initiative included the growing importance of warehouse receipts in supply chain and value chain financing; constraints in access to credit limiting economic growth, particularly in developing countries and emerging markets; a lack of norms governing warehouse receipts in many jurisdictions; and the need to harmonize existing standards on warehouse receipts promoted by international organizations.

157. On 26 March 2020, UNCITRAL and UNIDROIT organized a joint webinar on the proposal to develop a Model Law on Warehouse Receipts. The webinar gathered input from a multidisciplinary group of experts from various geographic regions representing academia, stakeholders, institutional actors, and international organizations active in the field. Its conclusions and recommendations confirmed the desirability and potential benefits of a Model Law endorsed at international level. At its 99th session (April/May 2020), the UNIDROIT Governing Council approved the project for the 2020–2022 Work Programme as a high-priority project, as did the UNCITRAL Commission at its 53rd session in September 2020. Two phases were envisaged for the preparation of the Model Law: first, the development of a comprehensive draft Model Law on Warehouse Receipts by an UNIDROIT Working Group (Phase I, 2020–2022); secondly, once completed, the draft Model Law should be submitted to a UNCITRAL Working Group for intergovernmental negotiations (Phase II). The Model Law should consist of a set of black-letter rules covering the private law aspects of a warehouse receipt system, contemplating:

(1) the issuance and transfer of electronic warehouse receipts, including through the use of electronic platforms;
(2) distributed ledger technology (DLT) systems; and
(3) other technological mechanisms.

158. A Working Group for Phase I was consequently set up. It held six sessions (2–4 December 2020, 10–12 March 2021, 1–3 September 2021, 28 February–2 March 2022, 5–7 December 2022 and 1–3 March 2023).

159. It had been envisaged that, upon the project's completion, consideration would be given to complementary work on a guide to enactment, including commentaries on the model provisions and on the legislation necessary to implement the Model Law at country level. At its 101st session (2022), the Governing Council authorized the extension of the project for an additional calendar year to permit the preparation of a Guide to Enactment of the Model Law. It was agreed that, in light of the joint nature of the project, the drafts of both the Model Law and the Guide to Enactment would be transmitted to UNCITRAL for intergovernmental negotiation and approval by the Commission. The recommendation by the Governing

Council to retain the project in the 2023–2025 Work Programme as a high-priority activity until its final completion, (2023 for the text of the Model Law, 2024 for the Guide to Enactment) was endorsed by the General Assembly at its 2022 session.

Chapter 13. Digital Assets and Private Law

160. In 2015, the Hungarian Ministry of Justice proposed that UNIDROIT develop model laws in the domain of 'business informatics'. This was followed in 2016 and 2018 by the Ministry of Industry and Trade of the Czech Republic proposing that UNIDROIT include in its 2020–2022 Work Programme topics relating to DLT (including blockchain) and the inheritance of digital properties. A similar proposal relating to the legal aspects of smart contracts and artificial intelligence was presented to UNCITRAL. It was decided that the two organizations should explore these domains together to identify specific areas in which work could be undertaken. To this end, UNCITRAL and UNIDROIT organized two joint workshops, in May 2019 and March 2020 respectively. The UNIDROIT General Assembly, at its 78th session (2019), approved the inclusion of a project in the area of artificial intelligence, smart contracts and DLT in the 2020–2022 Work Programme. Following the mandate received, the Secretariat further refined the scope of the project presenting a proposal focusing on Digital Assets and Private Law. At its 99th session in September 2020, the UNIDROIT Governing Council approved the insertion of the project in the 2020–2022 Work Programme. An UNIDROIT Working Group was established to develop a legal instrument containing principles and legislative guidance in the area of private law and digital assets. Seven meetings of the Working Group were held, on 17–19 November 2020, 16–18 March 2021, 30 June–2 July 2021, 2–4 November 2021, 7–9 March 2022, 31 August–2 September 2022, 19 to 21 December 2022, and 8 to 10 March 2023 respectively. A public consultation was held on the Draft Principles and Commentary on Digital Assets and Private Law prepared by the Working Group in sessions 1–7, with comments being requested by 20 January 2023. The draft and comments thereon were examined by the Working Group at its eighth session.

161. In essence, the purpose of the project is to provide legislative guidance and to develop principles relating to the legal nature, transfer and use of digital assets. This should include a legal taxonomy of digital assets and an analysis focusing on proprietary interests, while considering specific issues arising in various contexts, such as secured transactions, applicable law in cross-border transactions, insolvency, and the legal position of intermediaries. The principles identified should embody best practices and international standards and enable jurisdictions to take a common approach to legal issues arising from the transfer and use of digital assets.

162. Important aspects of the Digital Assets and Private Law project involve, *inter alia*, a legal analysis of the holding, transfer, and taking of security over digital assets, issues relating to the provision of digital asset custody services, and issues relating to the insolvency of the custodian of digital assets. These items link with the UNIDROIT Convention on Substantive Rules for Intermediated Securities (2013) and the UNIDROIT Legislative Guide on Intermediated Securities (2017), as well as with the projects on Best Practices of Effective Enforcement, which has the analysis of the impact of new technologies on enforcement as one of its main objectives, and the joint UNIDROIT–UNCITRAL project for the preparation of a Model Law on

Warehouse Receipts, which examines the issuance and transfer of electronic warehouse receipts for goods stored in warehouses. Moreover, should the work on the drafting of a Model Law on Factoring cover receivables issued in the form of digital assets, the cross-fertilization between the projects would bring about important benefits.

Chapter 14. Bank Insolvency (Study LXXXIV)

163. The Secretariat received two separate proposals on the harmonization of rules in cases of the insolvency of a bank, one from the Bank of Italy, the other from the European Banking Institute (EBI). Following the 2008 global financial crisis, the international financial community joined forces to protect the banking and financial sectors from contagion and risk. These efforts resulted in a revamp of the legal infrastructure for the international banking system, although where financial distress concerned a bank that was too small to cause systemic damage, or an already insolvent financial institution which needed to be liquidated without any additional resolution, there existed neither a set of international standards nor a mechanism for adequate coordination and cooperation. This last stage relating to bank liquidation was left to domestic legislation, which often differs substantially from country to country.

164. The Secretariat proposed that the Governing Council approve the inclusion of the subject in the new Work Programme, covering, at least: the most efficient institutional mechanism for bank liquidation (e.g., judicial system versus administrative model, or a hybrid system); the type of powers that ought to be assigned to the court/administrative authority; the entry gate to liquidation proceedings and its coordination with banking resolution systems; which rules of general corporate insolvency proceedings should apply to the liquidation of banks; and the rules coordinating national courts/administrative authorities in cross-border cases. Other aspects which could be envisaged included outside liquidation and, from the standpoint of resolution measures, international standard and coordination mechanisms concerning the domestic system of priorities in insolvency and its relationship with bail-in rules ('no creditor worse off' principle and Total Loss Absorbing Capacity (TLAC) rules); aspects of recognition of resolution measures; and the mechanisms for recognition of contractual clauses that subject banks to resolution systems. At its 98th session, the Governing Council recommended that the General Assembly include the project in the Work Programme and assign it a medium priority, pending further research and a more defined scope for the project. At the 99th session of the Governing Council, the project was confirmed with medium priority, allowing the Secretariat to conduct a feasibility study to be submitted to the Governing Council at its 100th session. The Council examined the feasibility study and approved the proposed scope of the project, subject to existing regulatory standards and stressing its focus on smaller banks; recommended upgrading the project to high priority; and authorized the Secretariat to establish a Working Group. At the time of writing (March 2023), the Working Group has met three times (13–14 December 2021, 11–13 April 2022 and 17–19 October 2022). At the third session, the work conducted so far, also by the three subgroups set up at the first session (Subgroup 1 on Scope and Definitions; Objectives; Institutional models; Procedural and operational aspects; Subgroup 2 on Preparation; Grounds for opening insolvency proceedings; Tools; Funding; Subgroup 3 on Safeguards; Cross-border aspects; Group dimension; Creditor hierarchy; Financial contracts) was examined. The Working Group agreed to retain the three Subgroups, primarily for the analysis of the responses received to a comprehensive cross-jurisdictional survey conducted within the Working Group on relevant aspects of, and experiences with, bank liquidation regimes worldwide; to establish a Drafting Committee, which would be entrusted with the preparation of a first draft of the Guide; and to organize virtual intersessional meetings on specific issues, if needed.

Chapter 15. Transport

§1. International Carriage of Goods by Road (CMR) (Study XXIII)

165. Of the Conventions that originated with Unidroit but were subsequently brought to completion in other organizations, the most successful is, without doubt, the 1956 Geneva Convention on the Contract for the International Carriage of Goods by Road, more commonly known by its French acronym 'CMR' (*Convention relative au contrat de transport international de marchandises par route*).

166. Work on what was to become the CMR was completed at the United Nations Economic Commission for Europe (ECE). It was largely the work of a Committee of Experts set up jointly by Unidroit, the International Road Transport Union (IRU), and the International Chamber of Commerce (ICC). The draft convention was prepared by the Committee on the basis of the work previously conducted within Unidroit and on the 1890 International Convention on the Transport of Goods by Rail (known as the CIM in its 1970 version). It was taken over by the ECE acting through a Working Party which was a subsidiary of the ECE Inland Transport Committee.[81]

167. The CMR is one of the most successful conventions the preparation of which Unidroit has been involved in. It is used daily by carriers in Europe and beyond, the States having ratified it now, including also States such as Morocco and Iran. Furthermore, it has been taken as a model for the 2003 Uniform Act on Contracts for the carriage of goods by road adopted by the OHBLA as well as for the 1989 Inter-American Convention on Contracts for the International Carriage of Goods by Road. Its application has furthermore been extended to domestic carriage by road in a number of countries.

168. In 2008, an Additional Protocol to the CMR concerning the Electronic Consignment Note was adopted in Geneva by the ECE. The Protocol permits the use of electronic consignment notes.

169. Unidroit's involvement with the work on what was to become the Electronic Consignment Note Protocol began because, at its 78th Session (1999), the Governing Council was seized of a request for comments from the ECE on the problems concerning the exchange of electronic data in the framework of the CMR. This request had been made following an intervention by the IRU, which had suggested that the problems might best be solved by means of an additional Protocol to the CMR and that Unidroit, as the organization within which the CMR had originated, should take part in the process.

81. *See* M. Clarke, *International Carriage of Goods by Road: CMR*, 6th ed. (London, 2014), and Hill & Messent, *CMR: Contracts for the International Carriage of Goods by Road*, ed. A. Messent & D.A. Glass, 3rd ed. (London & Hong Kong, 2000).

170. The Governing Council decided that the Secretariat should reply to the ECE and the IRU that UNIDROIT accepted to participate in the work, even if the existing financial commitments of the organization would not permit it to give priority to the subject. This collaboration continued, with UNIDROIT being represented in meetings by Mr Jacques Putzeys, member of the Governing Council (1993–2003) and submitting a proposed text of the future Protocol. This proposal as well as another alternative proposal submitted by one of the ECE and UNIDROIT Member States was extensively discussed at the Working Party on Road Transport (SC.1) of the Transport Division of the ECE. In the end, a proposal presented jointly by Mr Putzeys as the representative of UNIDROIT and Mr José Angelo Estrella Faria, at the time officer of UNCITRAL, the assistance of which had been enlisted, was accepted and the new Protocol adopted on 20 February 2008 in Geneva.

§2. Transport in General (Study LXXVII)

171. The idea of preparing a model law or principles in the field of transport law in general was put forward in 1998 by a correspondent of the Institute who suggested that such an international instrument might, for example, usefully be prepared with a view to assisting States to transpose the rules of the CMR into their domestic legislation, as such a transposition was not simply a matter of incorporating the text of the CMR as it stood. Albeit arousing interest, work was not initiated on this proposal.

§3. Liability of International Terminal Operators (Study XLIV)

172. The origins of what was to become the 1991 Convention on the Liability of Operators of Transport Terminals (OTT), which was finalized and adopted by UNCITRAL are to be found in the work conducted by UNIDROIT on bailment and warehousing contracts, a subject that had been included in the Work Programme of the Institute in 1960 in the context of combined transport operations, as particular problems arose in that context from the lack of uniform rules on the liability of persons into whose custody goods were entrusted before, during or after the actual transport of the goods.[82] At its 56th Session (1977), the Governing Council decided to set up a Study Group to draw up uniform rules on the warehousing contract. By 1982, the Study Group had prepared a preliminary draft convention on the liability of operators of transport terminals which was approved by the Governing Council at its 62nd session in 1983.[83]

82. United Nations Conference on the Liability of Operators of Transport Terminals in International Trade, Vienna, 2–19 Apr. 1991 (Official records, United Nations, New York, 1993), 24 – Background to the Draft Convention on the Liability of Operators of Transport Terminals in International Trade, Document A /CONF.152 /6, para. 1.

83. *Ibid.*, para. 2.

173. In the meantime, UNCITRAL, by reason of the close relationship between the draft developed by UNIDROIT and the international conventions relating to the carriage of goods, in particular, the 1978 United Nations Convention on the Carriage of Goods by Sea prepared by UNCITRAL, and the relevance of the subject to the needs of a number of developing countries, communicated the interest of the Commission to work on the subject to the Governing Council of UNIDROIT. UNIDROIT decided that it was interested in cooperating with the Commission on this topic and this was duly transmitted to the Commission.[84] UNCITRAL thereafter requested UNIDROIT to transmit its preliminary draft convention to the Commission for its consideration and set up a Working Group to work on the subject.[85] The Convention was finalized by UNCITRAL and adopted at a Conference held in Vienna in April 1991.

84. United Nations Conference on the Liability of Operators of Transport Terminals in International Trade, Vienna, 2–19 Apr. 1991 (Official records, United Nations, New York, 1993), 24 – Background to the Draft Convention on the Liability of Operators of Transport Terminals in International Trade, Document A /CONF.152 /6, para. 3.

85. *Ibid.*, para. 4.

Chapter 16. Civil Liability for Damage Caused During the Carriage of Dangerous Goods by Road, Rail and Inland Navigation Vessels (Study LV)

174. In 1972, the Government of the Netherlands requested that an item concerning the feasibility of preparing an international Convention relating to civil liability for damage caused as a consequence of the carriage of hazardous substances be included in the UNIDROIT Work Programme. In 1974, the subject was duly entered into the Work Programme for the triennium 1975–1977, but without priority, in view on the one hand of the fact that the Programme was already overloaded and on the other of a parallel initiative of the Netherlands Government within the ECE, which led to the transmission to the Member States of the Commission of a questionnaire concerning a number of aspects of the legal rules pertaining to civil liability for damage caused during the carriage of hazardous substances by road.[86] The results of the enquiry were analysed by the Dutch Government and thereafter submitted to the Working Party on Road Transport of the ECE Inland Transport Committee. This body noted that similar problems existed in connection with other modes of transport and it was agreed that the document should be transmitted to the members of the Working Parties on Rail and Inland Water Transport.

175. In February 1976, the Inland Transport Committee decided to ask UNIDROIT to undertake a preliminary study regarding the possibility of preparing a draft convention on third-party liability for damage caused during the carriage of hazardous substances by road, which would aim at establishing 'a uniform international application of the principle of third-party responsibility (whether limited or not) of the carrier and possibly the appropriate procedures for obtaining compensation'.[87] The Governing Council of UNIDROIT agreed at its 58th session in September 1979 that the study should be prepared by the UNIDROIT Secretariat, although its scope was extended, in accordance with the wishes of the Governments of France and the Netherlands, to cover damage caused during the carriage of hazardous substances by rail and inland waterway. In conformity with a decision taken by the Governing Council at its 59th session in May 1980, the study was submitted for consideration to an UNIDROIT Committee of Governmental Experts.[88] It was a rare occasion on which the Study Group stage was omitted and work passed directly to a Committee of Governmental Experts. The Committee met seven times. After the

86. Economic Commission for Europe, Convention on Civil Liability for Damage caused during carriage of Dangerous Goods by Road, Rail and Inland Navigation Vessels (CRTD) – Explanatory Report (United Nations, New York, 1990), 1, para. 1. This paragraph and the following are taken from the Explanatory Report, which contains a summary of the background to the Convention. The Explanatory Report was prepared by Mr Malcolm Evans, at the time Secretary-General of UNIDROIT, at the request of the ECE.

87. ECE documents TRANS 18, para. 90 and TRANS/SC1/284, paras 64 and 65.

88. ECE, Explanatory Report, *supra*, 1–2, paras 2 and 3.

draft had been finalized, it was transmitted to the ECE for finalization. The Convention on Civil Liability for Damage caused during Carriage of Dangerous Goods by Road, Rail and Inland Navigation Vessels (CRTD) was finally adopted in 1989. It is not yet in force.

176. Article 2 of the Convention specifies that it 'shall apply: (a) to damage sustained in the territory of a State Party and caused by an incident occurring in a State Party; (b) to preventive measures, wherever taken, to prevent or minimize such damage'. Articles 3 and 4 continue specifying further when the Convention applies and when it does not, before the Convention turns to the liability provisions (Articles 5–8) and to the provisions that limit liability (Articles 9–12), compulsory insurance (Articles 13–17), and claims and actions (Articles 18–31).

177. As indicated above, the Convention is not yet in force. The ECE took up work on the CRTD again in 2002, setting up an Ad hoc Meeting of Experts on the CRTD. The Ad hoc Meeting held four sessions in 2002 and 2003. A new text (the 'New CRTD') was drawn up, with certain modifications to the original text, *inter alia*, the reference to 'Inland Navigation Vessels' was replaced by a reference to 'inland waterway'. The new text was submitted to the Inland Transport Committee of the ECE in 2004.

Chapter 17. Form of an International Will (Study XLIII)

178. The 1973, Convention on the Form of an International Will was adopted at a Diplomatic Conference held in Washington 16–26 October 1973. Work on the project which was to lead to the Convention was begun in 1961, following the adoption of the Hague Convention of 5 October 1961 on the Conflicts of Laws Relating to the Form of the Clauses of a Will. Shortly before the Washington Diplomatic Conference, the Convention on the Establishment of a Scheme of Registration of Wills, drawn up within the framework of the Council of Europe, had been signed in Basel (16 May 1972). As is observed in the Explanatory Report to the Convention:

> [t]he rules on testamentary succession […] vary considerably in the different national legal systems, these rules and practices often being deeply rooted in tradition. […] the spectacular increase in the mobility of persons and goods, as a result of developments in the means of communication and transport and in international trade, has accentuated the drawbacks resulting from these differences.[89]

179. In 1960, the Governing Council of UNIDROIT decided to consider whether there might not be a possibility of making further progress beyond the provisions agreed on at the Hague in 1961, and to examine whether it might not be possible, by going one step further, to agree on a certain form of will acceptable to the internal law of every country. It was with this in mind that a Working Committee was convened by UNIDROIT in 1961 to draw up a preliminary draft of a uniform law introducing a new form of will, the 'international will'.

180. As is indicated in the Explanatory Report:

> [t]he provisions of the Uniform Law deal only with form in the strict sense: all questions which may in certain respects relate to rules of substance such as the personal capacity required of the testator or of the witnesses, the joint will, have been left aside, as have questions relating to the revocation, destruction or modification of wills. […].[90]

It continues:

> it was the intention of the authors of the Convention to give priority to the testator's discretion and respect for his intentions over any form requirements unnecessary to guarantee the real intentions of the testator. This is why the Uniform Law prescribes two classes of formality: those that are prescribed on pain of the international will being declared void (Arts. 2–5) and those for which, on the contrary, there is no penalty for non-compliance. The first provide the essential safeguards deemed to be necessary for the testator's protection. The

89. J.P. Plantard, 'Explanatory Report on the Convention providing a Uniform Law on the Form of an International Will', *Uniform Law Review* (1974): 91, 93.
90. *Ibid.*, 95.

others were laid down for their practical convenience and in order to bring about a more thorough unification; however, these objectives were judged to be of minor importance by comparison with the faithful carrying out of the testator's wishes. […] What is chiefly original and of interest in this Convention is this direct recognition of the formal validity of all international wills by each national law without any distinction being drawn between those drawn up in the country where the judge is sitting and those drawn up abroad on condition that the formal requirements laid down by Articles 2 to 5 of the Uniform Law have been respected. This direct assessment of the formal regularity of an act carried out abroad by reference to national law is an innovation which deserves to be underlined.[91]

91. *Ibid.*, 97.

Chapter 18. Cultural Property (Study LXX)

§1. The 1995 Unidroit Convention on Stolen or Illegally Exported Cultural Objects

181. The work Unidroit conducted in relation to cultural property undertook at the request of the United Nations Organization for Education, Science, and Culture (UNESCO) when the time came for the latter to adopt rules to implement its 1970 Convention on the Means of Prohibiting and Preventing the Illicit Import, Export, and Transfer of Ownership of Cultural Property. Thus, at the request of UNESCO, the Governing Council at its 65th session, in April 1986, decided to include the subject of the international protection of cultural property in the Work Programme of the Institute.[92] The final text of the Unidroit Convention on Stolen or Illegally Exported Cultural Objects was adopted at a Diplomatic Conference held in Rome in May 1995.

182. The starting point for Unidroit's work was Article 7(b)(ii) of the 1970 Convention and concentrated on the theft and illegal export of cultural property which were the situations dealt with in that provision. It should be pointed out that the two conventions deal with exactly the same categories of objects, which are those which 'on religious or secular grounds, are of importance for archaeology, prehistory, history, literature, art or science and belong to one of the categories listed in the Annex to this Convention'.[93]

183. The aim as is evinced from the Preamble of the Convention:

> is to establish 'common, minimal legal rules' in as many States as possible so as to prevent traffickers from exploiting differences between legal systems. The Convention also aims at providing remedies such as compensation, failing which the mechanism for restitution or return would be unacceptable to some States, but without making them binding on those States that see no need for them […] the new instrument in no way claims to offer an exclusive remedy for the problem of trafficking: on the contrary, stress is laid on the need for further measures such as the development and use of registers or the physical protection of archaeological sites. Finally, the Preamble calls for steps to strengthen international co-operation and to guarantee proper conditions for lawful trade in cultural objects.[94]

184. It should be noted that the Convention does not have a retroactive effect, even if the States adopting the Convention in the Preamble state that 'the adoption of the provisions of this Convention for the future in no way confers any approval

92. *See* 'Unidroit Convention on Stolen or Illegally Exported Cultural Objects: Explanatory Report Prepared by the Unidroit Secretariat, in English and French', *Uniform Law Review* (2001): 476–581.
93. Article 2.
94. *See* 'Unidroit Convention on Stolen or Illegally Exported Cultural Objects: Explanatory Report Prepared by the Unidroit Secretariat, in English and French', *Uniform Law Review* (2001): 490.

or legitimacy upon illegal transactions of whatever kind which may have taken place before the entry into force of the Convention'. It is up to States to reach bilateral agreements to solve situations that have arisen prior to the entry into force of the Convention.

185. In effect, as is indicated in the Explanatory Report, the Convention represents a compromise which attempts to reconcile two opposing positions:

> the advocates of the free movement of cultural objects worldwide who sought to restrict as far as possible the substantive scope of application of the Convention and to preserve the protection at present enjoyed in their countries by the purchaser in good faith; and the partisans of national protection of the cultural heritage who wished to extend as far as possible the principle of the return of stolen or illegally exported cultural objects and thereby to obtain the maximum level of international protection for their national cultural heritage.[95]

Needless to say, feelings run high where cultural property is concerned, and the art dealers' lobby in several countries has taken stands against the Convention for fear it may result in the inhibition of the art market. Clearly, the intention of the Convention is to inhibit the illegal trade in art objects, not the legitimate trade.

§2. Model Provisions on State Ownership of Undiscovered Cultural Objects (Study LXX A)

186. In 2009, the UNESCO Intergovernmental Committee for Promoting the Return of Cultural Property to its Countries of Origin or its Restitution in case of Illicit Appropriation decided to request the Secretariats of UNESCO and UNIDROIT to create a committee of independent experts entrusted 'with the task of preparing a model law that defines States' property rights, particularly those regarding archaeological heritage, that could assist in the drafting of national laws and encourage uniform terminology, considering not only legal aspects, but also ethical, philosophical and historical aspects […]'. The Governing Council of UNIDROIT agreed in principle to collaborate with UNESCO on the preparation of an instrument, tentatively a model law, to facilitate both the application of the 1970 UNESCO Convention and the 1995 UNIDROIT Convention and their ratification by as many States as possible.

187. The end product was not a model law, but Model Provisions which were adopted in 2011. They are intended to assist domestic bodies in the establishment of a normative framework for heritage protection, in the adoption of effective legislation for the establishment and recognition of the State's ownership of undiscovered cultural objects with a view, *inter alia*, to facilitate restitution in cases of unlawful removal. They are accompanied by guidelines for a better understanding of the provisions.

95. *Ibid.*, 482.

§3. Private Art Collections (Study LXX B)

188. In October 2015, the Permanent Mission of Mexico to the International Organizations in Rome transmitted to the Secretariat a document containing a proposal for work on legal issues related to private art collections. The purpose is to create international norms which would allow States to choose which cultural objects from private art collections should be protected. The proposal had been triggered by recent developments: first, the emergence of several recent cases involving privately held cultural property; second, recent legislation that protected and preserved national, cultural items; and third, adjudications which involved contracts between public museums and private art collections.

189. The Governing Council decided to recommend to the General Assembly that this topic be included in the Unidroit Work Programme for the 2017–2019 triennium but to assign it a low level of priority. The General Assembly endorsed this recommendation at its 75th session, on 1 December 2016.

190. On 16 and 17 March 2017, Unidroit hosted a conference on Private Collections: Historical and Legal Perspectives. The Conference was organized jointly with the International Society of Research and Cultural Heritage Law (ISCHAL), the *Institut des sciences sociales du politique* (*CNRS-ENS Cachan-Université Paris-Nanterre*) and BonelliErede law firm. A document derived from the findings of the conference indicating private law aspects on which Unidroit's particular expertise would be of additional benefit in this field was submitted to the Governing Council in May 2017 by Professor Elina Moustaira, Professor of Comparative Law at the School of Law of the National and Kapodistrian University of Athens. The Governing Council decided to recommend that the General Assembly include the topic of Private Art Collections in the Unidroit Work Programme for the 2017–2019 triennium with a low level of priority. The General Assembly endorsed this recommendation at its 75th session (1 December 2016). Unidroit has continued monitoring developments in the field, participating in meetings and conferences relevant to the topic. In 2021, it organised a colloquium together with the University of Geneva and the Gandur Foundation for Art in Geneva, entitled 'What prospects for "orphan works"? Reflections on Cultural Goods without Provenance' (Geneva, 4–5 February 2021). As part of the Work Programme for the triennial period 2023–2025, the Council at its 101st session (8–10 June 2022) proposed that the General Assembly at its 81st session (9 December 2022) increase the priority of the project to medium and that a Working Group to address orphan cultural objects be set up. It also decided that work should start with a smaller Working Group. A first online meeting of an Exploratory Expert Group was therefore held (12 September 2022), with a second meeting being scheduled for March 2023.

Chapter 19. Third-Party Liability for Global Navigation Satellite System (GNSS) Services (Study LXXIX)

191. At the 85th session of the Governing Council in 2006, the President of UNIDROIT informed the Council of a proposal he had received suggesting that the Institute might envisage including a project on third-party liability for services provided by satellite navigation systems (GNSS) in its Work Programme: a failure or malfunctioning of a GNSS might cause damage that could become a source of civil liability. As in many areas of activity with global impact (i.e., transport, nuclear activities, pollution), an international uniform legal discipline for GNSS might address a whole range of different problems (jurisdiction, difficulty of identifying the responsible party, effective loss restoration mechanisms, coordination with existing convention regimes).

192. The proposal met with divided opinions. While some considered the problems raised to be of local impact and therefore best dealt with by bodies such as the EU, others felt the topic to be of extreme importance and of global impact. A number of documents were submitted to the Council in the following years, the most comprehensive and analytical being the study prepared by the Secretariat at the request of the Council and submitted to it at its 89th session in 2010.[96] Following the discussion of this document, the Council invited the Secretariat to conduct informal consultations with the Governments and other organizations concerned, with a view to ascertaining the feasibility of the project.

193. Three informal meetings with States, organizations, and experts were held in order to elicit information on the desirability and feasibility of the preparation of an international instrument on civil liability for GNSS malfunctioning. It was decided to postpone taking a final decision until the EU had taken a decision on whether or not it would proceed with the preparation of a Regulation in this matter, a decision based on an Impact Assessment which was never published.

96. *See* document C.D.(89) 7 Add. 1.

Chapter 20. Private Law and Development (Study LXXX)

194. A new area of activity proposed by the Secretary-General is that of private law and development. The ultimate purpose is to contribute to the realization of the Development Goals set by the United Nations. Two specific topics were originally identified: private law aspects of agricultural financing and social enterprises, a document on each being submitted to the Governing Council at its 89th session in 2010. Subsequently, whereas the subject of social enterprises was put on hold, awaiting the decisions of the International Development Law Organization (IDLO) with which this project was to be conducted, the subject of contract farming was identified as most promising.

§1. Private Law Aspects of Agricultural Financing

195. The document on private law aspects of agricultural financing observed that when agricultural financing is considered, the experience of the organization in the development of financing instruments should be brought to fruition. UNIDROIT might, therefore, usefully examine the possibility of assisting legislators and policymakers modernize or enhance the domestic legal framework for investment in agricultural production.

196. The general debate on agricultural Foreign Direct Investment (FDI) had not given much attention to the different fields of private law that affect investment decisions, financing, and marketing mechanisms for agricultural commodities in most countries, that promote sustainable agricultural investment, facilitate the mobilization of capital for rural enterprises, or favour rational and efficient choices for the marketing of agricultural commodities. Key measures of legal and institutional reforms could, therefore, include legal and institutional reforms to broaden the range of assets that can be used as collateral, including movable assets such as equipment, livestock, crops, inventory, and receivables. While other organizations had worked on a number of specific issues, so far the results of all of the instruments produced, studies and guidance documents, as they applied in particular to the private law aspects of transactions in the agricultural sector, had not been coordinated and produced in a coherent whole. The preparation of an international guidance document, possibly in the form of a legislative guide, might provide a useful addition to the wealth of specific advice already available. The project might also benefit from the collaboration of UNIDROIT with the Food and Agriculture Organization of the United Nations (FAO) and the International Fund for Agricultural Development (IFAD), both of which were based in Rome and had expressed interest in the project.

197. The Council examined the document submitted to it and decided to recommend the inclusion of work on private law aspects of agricultural financing in the

Work Programme for the triennium 2011–2013 to the General Assembly.[97] The General Assembly at its 67th session in 2010 endorsed this recommendation.

§2. CONTRACT FARMING (STUDY LXXX A)

198. In November 2011, UNIDROIT organized a colloquium on 'Promoting Investment in Agricultural Production: Private Law Aspects' which, with the consultations that had been conducted with the United Nations international agricultural development agencies, the FAO and IFAD, formed the basis of the realization by the Governing Council that UNIDROIT could usefully contribute its contract law expertise to the development of contract farming by preparing a legal guide on contract farming operations. It was consequently decided that attention should turn to contract farming, for which a legal guide in the form of a joint project with the FAO and IFAD, should be prepared. A Working Group was consequently set up. The Working Group held four sessions to finalise the draft Legal Guide (28–31 January 2013, 3–6 June 2013, 3–7 March 2014 and 17–21 November 2014). The final draft was approved by the UNIDROIT Governing Council at its 94th session (6–8 May 2015) and published later the same year.

199. The Guide is intended to offer a thorough analysis of substantive law issues that are involved in contract farming, identifying problem areas and possible solutions in light of trade usages and legislation.

§3. LEGAL GUIDE ON AGRICULTURAL LAND INVESTMENT CONTRACTS (ALIC) (STUDY LXXX B)

200. In 2012, the Governing Council authorized the Secretariat to pursue consultations and preliminary work with a view to the possible preparation of an international guidance document on land investment contracts, taking into account, in particular, the UNIDROIT Principles of International Commercial Contracts. Several international initiatives underway touched upon this area, most notably the preparation by FAO of the Principles for Responsible Investment in Agriculture and Foods Systems ('RAI Principles').

201. Following the adoption of the Legal Guide on Contract Farming at its 94th session in 2015, the Governing Council instructed the Secretariat to prepare a feasibility study on land investment contracts, in order to decide whether UNIDROIT's particular expertise would be of additional benefit in this field.

202. The feasibility study was submitted to the Governing Council at its 95th session. It indicated that, although other existing international instruments and policy papers contained important policy guidance on investments in land, UNIDROIT could use its private law expertise to build upon such instruments and

97. *See* document C.D.(89) 7 Misc. 4.

papers and prepare, in collaboration with the Rome-based food and agriculture organizations of the United Nations system and other institutions, valuable legal guidance for farmers, investors, Governments, and other stakeholders.

203. The Governing Council recommended that the General Assembly include the topic of an international guidance document on agricultural investment contracts in the UNIDROIT Work Programme for the 2017–2019 triennium. The General Assembly endorsed this recommendation at its 75th session, on 1 December 2016. A Working Group was set up and started to work the following year.

204. The Working Group met four times (3–5 May 2017, 13–15 September 2017, 25–27 April 2018 and 9–11 October 2018). At these meetings, discussions centred, in particular, on the notion of agricultural land investment contracts, the alignment of the work with existing initiatives, cooperation with FAO and IFAD, non-governmental organizations, civil society, the private sector and other stakeholders and the objective and target audience of the future instrument, including the scope, content and form of the instrument. At its fourth meeting, the Working Group agreed that the revised draft Guide (the 'ALIC Zero Draft') should be submitted to broad and extended consultations to raise awareness of the Legal Guide and to seek further input from stakeholders. This course of action was endorsed by the Governing Council at its 98th session (Rome, 8–10 May 2019).

205. The consultation process included both online consultations and regional consultations. Thus, from 1 June to 31 October 2019, the ALIC Zero Draft was made available for comment and feedback on the UNIDROIT website, as well as on a number of other key online platforms, including the Global Forum on Food Security and Nutrition (FSN Forum) hosted by FAO, the LandPortal.org, and the Afronomics law website. Three regional workshops were held in collaboration with IFAD and FAO in Beijing (9 July 2019), São Paulo (9 August 2019) and Nairobi (23 October 2019). The Drafting Committee (2–3 March 2020) reviewed the comments and recommendations received in the consultation process. At its 99th session, in September 2020, the UNIDROIT Governing Council approved the Legal Guide on Agricultural Land Investment Contracts, which was published as a joint UNIDROIT/IFAD publication.

§4. Legal Structure of Agricultural Enterprises (Study LXXX C)

206. At its 98th session (8–10 May 2019), the UNIDROIT Governing Council recommended the General Assembly include the preparation of a Guidance Document on the Legal Structure of Agricultural Enterprises (LSAE) in the 2020–2022 Work Programme. The General Assembly at its 78th session (12 December 2019) endorsed this recommendation.

207. In 2020, the Secretariat conducted a stocktaking exercise and feasibility study to ascertain whether the experience of UNIDROIT could be useful in this field. At the 99th session of the Council, the Secretariat, on the basis of the preliminary research conducted, confirmed that there was a lack of international guidance to best streamline supply chain relationships. The Secretariat also drew the Council's attention to the strong interest, in particular from economists, for UNIDROIT undertaking work on the private law aspects of the legal structure of agricultural enterprises to improve market access, to improve forms of coordination of agricultural enterprises, to ease access to critical resources and insurance, and to address unfair commercial practices.

208. On 15 and 16 April 2021, the Secretariat organized a Consultation Webinar together with FAO and IFAD to obtain further information on the topics that could potentially be covered by the Guidance Document. The conclusions and recommendations of the Webinar were presented to the Council at its 100th session in 2021. The Council accepted the Secretariat's proposals to upgrade the status of the project and thus set up a Working Group. The General Assembly endorsed the recommendation of the Council, allocating high-priority status to the LSAE project at its 80th session (December 2021).

209. On the occasion of the General Assembly meeting, on 9–10 December 2021, the Secretariat organized an informal exploratory meeting with a core group of experts to identify the topics and questions that needed to be further developed in an annotated issues paper to be submitted for discussion to the Working Group at its first session. The first session of the LSAE Working Group was held on 23–25 February 2022, and the second on 2–4 November 2022.

Chapter 21. Database on Uniform Law (UNILAW) (Study LXIX)

210. In 1993, UNIDROIT decided to examine the feasibility and desirability of setting up a database to permit ready access by Governments, judges, arbitrators, practising lawyers and scholars to up-to-date information on uniform law conventions and other instruments. The database was to be in both English and French.

211. Consideration of the establishment by UNIDROIT of a database on uniform law was for the first time seriously addressed in the context of the overall policy review of the Institute, the first findings under which the Secretariat submitted to the Governing Council at its 73rd session in May 1994.

212. As the technological revolution of the last three decades of the twentieth century advanced, UNIDROIT realized the potential importance of high-quality electronic systems, particularly of a uniform law information system or database. Many developed countries have databases offering information on domestic law – legislation and case law – but there are relatively few that deal in any systematic way with international law in general or with uniform private law in particular. Furthermore, no single institution has established itself as a focal point for the collection of at least the most important data on major uniform law topics. It was to fill this void that UNIDROIT decided to set up a database on uniform law. The UNIDROIT objective was to establish an electronic source of uniform law with authority and a guarantee of continuity in ultimately covering the whole reach of uniform law.

213. Work on the database progressed for a number of years, never being able to count on the resources necessary for such a project despite the support of the Uniform Law Foundation (now UNIDROIT Foundation). It was with regret that in 2012, work was discontinued as being too resource-intensive.

Chapter 22. Programme of Legal Cooperation (Study LXV)

214. An interest in this item first emerged at the Vth Meeting of the Organizations concerned with the Unification of Law, held in Rome under the auspices of UNIDROIT in 1973, one of the two main themes of which was 'Uniform Law as a Means of Technical Assistance to Developing Countries'. This subject was subsequently included by the Governing Council in the Work Programme for the period 1978–1980. In the following years, the Secretariat's efforts were concentrated on developing cooperation with a number of bodies with an interest in the question, the intention being to make UNIDROIT and its achievements more widely known and at the same time to contemplate joint action in the area of legal assistance pending the definition of a specific programme tailored to the Institute's resources.

215. At the Governing Council's 71st session in June 1992, UNIDROIT's original conception of legal assistance was enlarged so as to encompass not only developing countries but also countries engaged in the transition to a market economy, although it was fully appreciated that the problems facing the two groups of States differed considerably.

216. In addition to more specific recognition of the interests of those countries in the choice of the items retained on the UNIDROIT Work Programme with a view to the preparation of international instruments, and a wider distribution of the Institute's publications in those countries, the Council approved two principal forms of action proposed by the Secretariat, namely the holding of seminars *in loco* and a programme of research scholarships for lawyers from countries developing their economies or engaged in the process of the transition to a market economy, the funding of which would be met essentially from sources external to the general budget of UNIDROIT.

217. The programme of research scholarships offered by the Institute is designed to promote, for the benefit of lawyers (Government officials and academics) from developing countries and from countries engaged in the transition to a market economy, the statutory aims of UNIDROIT and is essentially determined by funds specifically obtained for that purpose. The scholars are admitted to the UNIDROIT Library for a period of, on average, two months, during which time they conduct research on a project previously submitted by them. In some cases, UNIDROIT scholarships are arranged in conjunction with additional periods spent at associate institutions located in Europe so as to permit the scholars to round off their training and to enlarge or pursue in greater depth their research and enrich their international experience.

218. A development of this Programme was the assistance offered by the organization to countries or regional integration groups intending to modernize or reform their legislation, in particular developing countries or countries in transition to a market economy, in legal drafting. A first instance of this activity was the mandate conferred upon UNIDROIT by the Council of Ministers of the OHBLA to offer its expertise with a view to the preparation of a draft uniform law on contract law in the light of the UNIDROIT Principles of International Commercial Contracts.

Chapter 23. The Foundation for the Support of UNIDROIT (Formerly the Uniform Law Foundation) (Study LXXIV)

219. Financial resources are a problem for all international organizations. Member States often have problems increasing their contributions to the organizations, which is not surprising considering the economic problems faced by all. With a view to solving this problem, a proposal was launched in the Governing Council for the creation of a Foundation that would provide funding for projects that the Institute considered meritorious but which it was not in a position to fund out of its ordinary budget, first and foremost the database on uniform law. This proposal resulted in the Secretariat's submitting to the Governing Council at its 74th session, a comparative survey of the regulation of foundations in ten countries, from which it appeared that the most appropriate location for the creation of a foundation or similar association was the Netherlands.

220. At its 75th session, held in June 1996, the Governing Council conferred upon the President of the Institute the mandate to take the necessary steps with a view to its creation. The Uniform Law Foundation was formally established in the Netherlands on 9 October 1996 by Mr Luigi Ferrari Bravo, at the time President of UNIDROIT and Judge at the International Court of Justice, and Mr Arthur Hartkamp, member of the UNIDROIT Governing Council and at the time Advocate-General at the Supreme Court of the Netherlands.

221. For a number of years, the Foundation remained inactive. In 2003, it was decided that an effort should be made to render it operative. Thanks to initial personal donations, initiatives were taken under the direction of its new President, Sir Roy Goode, with a view to initiating publicizing both the Foundation and the work of the Institute it should contribute to fund.

222. In 2013, the Presidency was taken over by Mr Jeffrey Wool of Freshfields Bruckhaus Deringer, Secretary-General of the AWG and Condon-Falknor Professor of Global Business Law at the University of Washington (USA). At the meeting of the Board of Governors that year, it was also decided that the Foundation would change its name to 'The Foundation for the Support of UNIDROIT (UNIDROIT Foundation)'.

Chapter 24. Subsidiary Activities

223. Essential support for UNIDROIT's core activity of the drawing up of uniform rules is provided by its maintenance of a world-renowned library, its preparation of a number of specialist publications in the field of the unification of law, its legal cooperation programme,[98] and by its periodic organization of congresses, meetings, and seminars.

§1. LIBRARY

224. The UNIDROIT Library is one of the leading documentation centres in its field and is consulted by researchers from all over the world. Its holdings include over 260,000 books and 450 current periodicals covering both a wide range of countries and all the different branches of private law, in particular commercial law, as well as private international law and comparative law. With a view to making information relating to these holdings accessible online, the library catalogue has been computerized.

225. UNIDROIT's activities in the field of the harmonization and unification of private law reflect on the type of publication collected, that is mainly publications and periodicals dealing with private law and, in particular, commercial law. The Library's collection of books and other documentation also comprises a wide selection of materials on international private law, international trade law, private comparative law, and international public law. Moreover, there are special sections on Roman and canon law and legal bibliography. The UNIDROIT Library maintains extensive collections of the documentation of international organizations such as the League of Nations, the UN, the ILO, the IMO, the Council of Europe, the OAS, the Nordic Council, and the Hague Conference on Private International Law.

I. The Gorla Collection

226. In 1987, Gino Gorla, formerly Professor of Comparative Law at the University of Rome I '*La Sapienza*', donated to the UNIDROIT Library, his collection of antique books which he had collected as support for his research on case law in Europe from the seventeenth to the early part of the nineteenth century. This collection of over 550 titles comprising about 900 volumes is composed of treatises, commentaries, collections of *decisiones*, *resolutiones*, *consilia*, *responsa*, *allegationes,* and *controversiae forenses*. The majority of the volumes were published in Italian cities, although many come from France, Spain, Germany, Belgium, England and the United States of America. Professor Gorla's collection also comprises a number of seventeenth to early nineteenth-century books dealing specifically with commercial law and maritime law.

---

98. *See* Ch. 19, *supra.*

§2. PUBLICATIONS

227. From its earliest days, UNIDROIT has issued a number of publications. A regular publication is the *Uniform Law Review/Revue de droit uniforme*, published on a quarterly basis since 1996, by Oxford University Press since 2013. It is a bilingual publication in English and French, comprising the following sections: articles; international developments (including a periodical review of UNIDROIT's own activities); and texts of new uniform law instruments. Some issues of the Uniform Law Review are mono-thematic, in that they publish the acts of conferences or congresses organized by UNIDROIT or other organizations or examine a specific project in detail. Others are celebratory: in 1998, the Uniform Law Review published a special double issue in memory of the late Secretary-General of UNIDROIT, Malcolm Evans.

A celebratory publication published by UNIDROIT in 2016, was the two volumes of Essays in honour of Professor Michael Joachim Bonell, a long-time collaborator and consultant to UNIDROIT as well as the chief promotor and coordinator of the Principles of International Commercial Contracts. The title of the publication is '*Eppur si muove:* The age of Uniform Law – Essays in honour of Michael Joachim Bonell, to celebrate his 70th birthday'. It comprises some 122 articles by 125 authors. In addition, 143 colleagues of Professor Bonell asked to be inserted in the *Tabula Gratulatoria* that opens the publication.

228. As many as 29 articles of the Essays in honour of Professor Bonell deal with the UNIDROIT Principles in one way or another but also other projects or instruments adopted by UNIDROIT are examined in the articles. As a whole, the articles cover: Personal Reminiscences; Legal Theory; Comparative Law, Transnational Law and Uniform Law in General: *(a) Comparative Law; (b) Transnational Law; (c) Uniform Law in General;* Private International Law; European Law: *(a) European Law in General; (b) European Private Law;* Contract Law: *(a) Comparative Contract Law; (b) International Contract Law; (c) UNIDROIT Principles of International Commercial Contracts;* Sales and Other Types of Contract: *(a) International Sales Contracts; (b) European Sales Contracts; (c) Other Types of Contract;* Company, Banking, Insolvency and Intellectual Property Law: *(a) Company Law; (b) Banking Law; (c) Insolvency Law; (d) Intellectual Property Law; Capital Markets; Property Law; Cultural Property; Succession; Arbitration and ADR;* and *Civil Procedure Law.*

229. In addition, UNIDROIT publishes monographs connected with its work, such as the *UNIDROIT Principles of International Commercial Contracts*, the four Official Commentaries by Professor Sir Roy Goode: the *Official Commentary on the Convention on International Interests in Mobile Equipment and Protocol thereto on Matters specific to Aircraft Equipment*, the *Official Commentary on the Convention on International Interests in Mobile Equipment and Luxembourg Protocol thereto on Matters specific to Railway Rolling Stock*, the *Official Commentary on the Convention on International Interests in Mobile Equipment and Protocol thereto on Matters specific to Space Assets,* and the *Official Commentary on the Convention on International Interests in Mobile Equipment and Protocol thereto on Matters*

Specific to Mining, Agricultural and Construction Equipment; the *Guide to International Master Franchise Arrangements,* the *UNIDROIT/FAO/IFAD Legal Guide on Contract Farming* and the *UNIDROIT/IFAD Legal Guide to Adricultural Land Investment Contracts..*

§3. CONGRESSES, MEETINGS, AND SEMINARS

230. UNIDROIT periodically organizes international congresses, meetings, and seminars to discuss topical aspects of the unification of law, such as methodology and its practical applications, whether to specific projects or in general. These events bring together judges, arbitrators, academics, and practising lawyers as well as national and international civil servants. As indicated above, the *Uniform Law Review* publishes the acts of some of the congresses organized by the Institute.

231. Previous general congresses include:

(1) The Fourth Congress on Private Law, Rome, 27–28 September 2002, on 'Worldwide Harmonisation of Private Law and Regional Economic Integration', organized to celebrate the 75th Anniversary of the Founding of UNIDROIT.
(2) The Third Congress on Private Law, Rome, 7–10 September 1987, on 'International Uniform Law in Practice'.
(3) The Second Congress on Private Law, Rome, 9–15 September 1976, on 'New Directions in International Trade Law'.
(4) The First Congress on Private Law, Rome, 8–16 July 1950.

232. In addition, UNIDROIT organizes congresses and conferences on special topics or for special events: to mark the 90th anniversary of the founding of UNIDROIT, in addition to more specific seminars, a special session of the General Assembly of the organization with an International Symposium on 'Private Law, International Cooperation and Development' was held on 20 April 2016. The more specific events included international congresses on 'Practicing International Law at the United Nations' (15 April 2016) and 'The League of Nations and UNIDROIT' (19 April 2016), as well as a Conference on 'Creating a favourable Legal Environment for Contract Farming' (27 April 2016) and an International Contract Law Conference in Cooperation with the CISG Advisory Council on the occasion of the 95th session of the UNIDROIT Governing Council on 'United Nations Convention on Contracts for the International Sale of Goods (CISG), UNIDROIT Principles of International Commercial Contracts: Contrasts and Convergence'(20 May 2016). Lastly, Professor Michael Joachim Bonell was presented with the two volumes of the Essays in his honour with the title '*Eppur si muove*: The age of Uniform Law Essays in honour of Michael Joachim Bonell, to celebrate his 70th birthday' (Rome, 29 September 2016) (*see* above).

§4. Depositary Libraries

233. With a view to making the documents issued by UNIDROIT more readily available in its Member States, the Member States were requested to designate a Depository Library to which the organization would send its documentation on a regular basis. Not all States designated a Depository Library, also in view of the fact that recent documentation is available on the website of the organization. A list of the depository libraries is to be found in Appendix 4.

§5. The Aftermath: Publicizing International Instruments

234. As is the case with all international organizations, it is important for UNIDROIT to promote knowledge of its instruments, to strike a balance between the drawing up of new uniform law instruments and the promotion of existing ones. To this end, in addition to organizing global congresses and conferences, the President of the Institute in 1995 proposed to the Governing Council that a series of regional Congresses be organized to give exposure to the work of UNIDROIT. The first of these Congresses, truly Pan-American in character, devoted to the UNIDROIT Principles of International Commercial Contracts, was held in Venezuela in November 1996. A large number of participants attended the Congress, the speakers coming from Argentina, Brazil, Canada, Chile, Colombia, Mexico, the United States of America, Uruguay, and Venezuela, as well as from Spain, France, and Italy.

235. A second congress was held in November 1998 in Argentina on the theme: 'International Commercial Contracts: The Work of UNIDROIT'. It was organized by the *Universidad Argentina de la Empresa* in Buenos Aires and was coordinated by Mr Julio César Rivera, Professor of Law at the *Universidad de Buenos Aires*. UNIDROIT's work on franchising agreements, the Principles of International Commercial Contracts, leasing contracts, and factoring contracts were introduced by members of the UNIDROIT Secretariat and commented on by eminent Argentinean academics and practitioners.

236. In Cairo in January 2000, two seminars were held, the first was an International Commercial Arbitration Seminar which focussed on the role of the UNIDROIT Principles of International Commercial Contracts in international arbitration, but which also dealt with the role of UNCITRAL in international commercial arbitration and international arbitration in the Arab world. This Seminar was sponsored by the Egyptian Minister of Justice, H.E. Counsellor Farouk Seif El Nasr, and by the Cairo Regional Centre for International Commercial Arbitration, in the person of its Director, Dr Mohamed Aboul-Enein. The second Seminar was a Joint National Seminar by the Ministry of Justice in Egypt and UNIDROIT and focussed on the UNIDROIT project on International Interests in Mobile Equipment and the UNIDROIT Convention on Stolen or Illegally Exported Cultural Objects. It was sponsored by the Ministry of Justice and was chaired by Dr Iskander Ghattas, Under-Secretary of the Ministry of Justice.

237. In 2004, a colloquium on the draft Rail Protocol was organized in Mexico entitled *The International Legal Regimen for the Taking of Security in High-Value Mobile Equipment. Possibilities and Challenges*, a colloquium organized by UNIDROIT, the OTIF, the OAS, and the RWG, in consultation with ICAO, under the auspices of the Government of Mexico and the Mexican Center of Uniform Law (Mexico City, 11–12 October 2004).

238. On 23–24 March 2014, a conference to launch the Arabic version of the 2010 UNIDROIT Principles of International Commercial Contracts was held at the Sultan Qaboos University of Muscat, Oman. The conference, which was held in English and Arabic, was supported by the Johns Hopkins University and The Protection Program, and organized in collaboration with Sultan Qaboos University and UNIDROIT.

Part IV. Cooperation with Other International Organizations

239. UNIDROIT maintains close ties of cooperation with other international organizations, both intergovernmental and non-governmental. Indeed, as regards intergovernmental organizations, the Statute of the organization specifies that the Governing Council 'may enter into relations with other intergovernmental organizations [...], in order to ensure cooperation in conformity with their respective aim'.[99] In many cases, cooperation agreements are concluded at inter-Secretariat level. Cooperation is particularly close with the Hague Conference on Private International Law and UNCITRAL, as well as with the IBA. Recently cooperation with the FAO and IFAD on contract farming has been and continues to be, particularly fruitful.

240. By reason of its expertise in the international unification of law, UNIDROIT is moreover at times commissioned by other organizations to prepare comparative law studies and/or draft Conventions designed to serve as the basis for the preparation and/or finalization of international instruments in those organizations. A list of the instruments initiated by UNIDROIT and finalized by other organizations can be found in Appendix 2, whereas details on a few of these are provided above (*see* Part III, the sections on International Carriage of Goods by Road (CMR) (Chapter 12 §1), Terminal Operators (Chapter 12 §3), Carriage of Dangerous Goods (Chapter 13)). This was particularly the case in the past, whereas in the last ten to fifteen years, there has been a tendency for UNIDROIT to complete the whole process, even when asked to undertake a project by another organization (*see* Part III, the section on Cultural Property (Chapter 15)).

99. Article 12*bis*.

Appendix 1. Studies Prepared by UNIDROIT

- Bills of exchange, Promissory notes, Cheques (Study I)
- Enforcement Abroad of Maintenance Obligations (+ Miscellaneous Family Law and Adoption) (Study II)
- International law on arbitration (Study III)
- International sale of goods (Study IV)
- Copyright, reconciling the Bern and the Havana Conventions (Study V)
- Standard publication contract (Study VI)
- Credit paper guarantees other than those on the instrument (Study VII)
- Copyright: '*Droit de suite*' (Study VIII)
- Unfair competition. Performers' rights (Study IX)
- Copyright adaptation of musical works for mechanical instruments (Study X)
- Copyright: Protection of motion picture production (Study XI)
- The Hotelkeeper's contract (Study XII)
- Insurance (Study XIII)
- Stock exchange, security transactions, etc. (Study XIV)
- International carriage (Study XV)
- Formation of contracts by correspondence (Study XVI)
  - Formation of contracts for the international sale of goods (Study XVI A)
  - Validity of contracts of international sale of goods (Study XVI B)
- Civil liability and compulsory insurance of motorists (Study XVII)
- Uniform rules for clearing houses (Study XVIII)
- Agency in the international sale of goods (Study XIX)
- International loans (Study XX)
- Legal status of women (Study XXI)
- Public calamity insurance (Study XXII)
- International carriage of goods by road (Study XXIII)
- Commission on the international sale or purchase of goods (Study XXIV)
- Arbitration between Governments and Individuals (Study XXV)
- Unification of legislation on corporations (Study XXVI)
- International carriage of goods on inland waterways (Study XXVII)
  - Inland navigation law: Shipowner's liability (Study XXVII A)
  - Inland navigation law: Assistance and salvage (Study XXVII B)
  - Inland navigation law: Attachment pendente lite (Study XXVII C)
  - Inland navigation law: In rem rights (Study XXVII D)

  - Inland navigation law: Carriage of passengers and luggage by inland waterways (Study XXVII E)
- Establishment (Study XXVIII)
- Civil procedure (Council of Europe) (Study XXIX)
- Basic Products (Study XXX)
- Carriage of goods by rail (Study XXXI)
- Electric power (Study XXXII)
- European corporations (Study XXXIII)
- Liability regime of carriers for personal damage caused to passengers (Study XXXIV)
  - Carriage of passengers and luggage by road (Study XXXIV A)
  - Unification of the law relating to liability of carriers (Study XXXIV B)
- Commercial paper (Bills of exchange and promissory notes) (Study XXXV)
- Forwarding agency contracts (Study XXXVI)
- Interpretation of uniform laws (Study XXXVII)
- Protection of cultural property in case of war (Study XXXVIII)
- Unification of provisions of law of private international law (Study XXXIX)
- Trust (Study XL)
- Unfair competition (Study XLI)
- Combined transport of goods (Study XLII)
- International form of will (1973 Convention on the Form of an International Will) (Study XLIII)
- Liability of international terminal operators (1991 UN Convention on the Liability of Operators of Transport Terminals (OTT)) (Study XLIV)
- Acquisition in good faith of corporeal movables (Study XLV)
- Institutions for collective investment in the Member States of the Council of Europe (Study XLVI)
- Travel agency contract CCV (Study XLVIII)
- Sales of movables by instalment and on credit in the member countries of the Council of Europe (Study XLIX)
- Principles of international commercial contracts (Study L)
  - Formulation of Principles of Reinsurance Contracts (Study L)
  - Model Clauses for the Use of the Unidroit Principles of International Commercial Contracts (Study L)
  - Tripartite Legal Guide to Uniform Legal Instruments in the Area of International Commercial Contracts (with a focus on sales) (Study L)
- Transport by pipelines (Study LI)
- Legal Status of air-cushion vehicles (hovercraft) (Study LII)
- Civil liability for damage caused by small craft (Study LIII)
- Civil liability for damage caused during the carriage of dangerous goods by road, rail and inland navigation vessels (1989 ECE Convention on Civil Liability for Damage caused during carriage of Dangerous Goods by Road, Rail and Inland Navigation Vessels (CRTD)) (Study LV)
- Carriage of live animals (Study LVI)
- Gold clauses in international conventions (Study LVII)
- Factoring (Study LVIII)

  - The 1988 UNIDROIT Convention on International Factoring (Study LVIII)
  - Factoring Model Law (Study LXVIIIA)
- The international financial leasing contract (Study LIX)
- The 1988 UNIDROIT Convention on International Financial Leasing (Study LIX)
  - The Model Law on Leasing (Study LIXA)
- Inspection agency contracts (Quality and quantity control of goods) (Study LX)
- Power of Attorney (Study LXIII)
- Civil liability connected with the carrying out of dangerous activities (Study LXIV)
- Programme of legal assistance to developing countries (Study LXV)
- Credit cards (Study LXVII)
- Franchising contracts (Study LXVIII)
  - The Guide to International Master Franchise Arrangements ((Study LXVIII)
  - The Model Franchise Disclosure Law (Study LXVIII)
- Organisation of an information system or data bank on uniform law (Study LXIX)
- International protection on cultural property (Study LXX)
  - The 1995 UNIDROIT Convention on Stolen or Illegally Exported Cultural Objects (Study LXX)
  - UNESCO–UNIDROIT Model Provisions on State Ownership of Undiscovered Cultural Objects (Study LXX A)
  - Private art collections (Study LXX B)
- Internal relations between principals and agents in the international sale of goods (Study LXXI)
- International interests in mobile equipment (Security Interests) (Study LXXII)
  - The 2001 Cape Town Convention on International Interests in Mobile Convention (2001) (Study LXXII)
  - Model law in the general field of secured transactions (Study LXXII A)
  - Work of international organisations in the field of personal property security (Study LXXII B)
  - International interests in mobile equipment: consideration of the legal and technical issues raised by the establishment of an international register (Study LXXII C)
  - Protocol to the Convention on International Interests in Mobile Equipment on Matters specific to Aircraft Equipment (2001) (Study LXXII D)
  - Luxembourg Protocol to the Convention on International Interests in Mobile Equipment on Matters specific to Railway Rolling Stock (2007) (Study LXXII H)
  - Protocol to the Convention on International Interests in Mobile Equipment on Matters specific to Space Assets (2012) (Study LXXII J)
  - Protocol to the Convention on International Interests in Mobile Equipment on Matters specific to mining, agricultural and construction equipment (2019) (Study LXXII K)
  - Protocol to the Convention on International Interests in Mobile Equipment on ships and maritime transport equipment (Study LXXII W)

Appendix 1. Studies Prepared by UNIDROIT

- Legal issues connected with software (Study LXXIII)
- The Foundation for the Support of UNIDROIT (Formerly the Uniform Law Foundation) (Study LXXIV)
- Promotion of UNIDROIT activities and instruments (in particular the Internet site) (Study LXXV)
- Civil Procedure (Study LXXVI)
  - ALI-UNIDROIT Principles of Transnational Civil Procedure (Study LXXVI)
  - Formulation of Regional Rules: ELI – UNIDROIT Model European Rules of Civil Procedure (Study LXXVI A)
  - Best Practices for Effective Enforcement (Study LXXVI B)
- Uniform rules applicable to transport (Study LXXVII)
- Transactions on Transnational and Connected Capital Markets (Study LXXVIII)
  - Substantive Rules regarding Intermediated Securities (The 2009 Geneva Convention on Substantive Rules for Intermediated Securities) (Study LXXVIII A)
  - Principles and rules capable of enhancing trading in securities in emerging markets (UNIDROIT Legislative Guide on Intermediated Securities) (Study LXXVIII B)
  - Operation of Close-out Netting Provisions (Principles on the Operation of Close-Out Netting Provisions) (Study LXXVIII C)
- Third party liability for Global Navigation Satellite System (GNSS) services (Study LXXIX)
- Private law and agricultural development (Study LXXX)
  - Preparation of a Legal Guide on Contract Farming (Study LXXX A)
  - Legal Guide on agricultural land investment contracts (ALIC) (Study LXXX B)
  - Legal Structure of Agricultural Enterprises (Study LXXX C)
  - Legal Aspects of Social Enterprises (Study LXXXI)
- Digital Assets and Private Law (Study LXXXII)
- Model Law on Warehouse Receipts (Study LXXXIII)
- Bank Insolvency (Study LXXXIV)

Appendix 2. Instruments Adopted or Prepared by UNIDROIT

UNIDROIT has over the years prepared over seventy studies and drafts. Many of these have resulted in international instruments, including the following international Conventions, all in force unless otherwise indicated, drawn up by UNIDROIT and adopted at diplomatic Conferences convened by Member States of the organization:

- 1964 Convention relating to a Uniform Law on the Formation of Contracts for the International Sale of Goods (The Hague);
- 1964 Convention relating to a Uniform Law on the International Sale of Goods (The Hague);
- 1970 International Convention on the Travel Contract (Brussels);
- 1973 Convention providing a Uniform Law on the Form of an International Will (Washington);
- 1983 Convention on Agency in the International Sale of Goods (Geneva);
- 1988 UNIDROIT Convention on International Financial Leasing (Ottawa);
- 1988 UNIDROIT Convention on International Factoring (Ottawa);
- 1995 UNIDROIT Convention on Stolen or Illegally Exported Cultural Objects (Rome);
- 2001 Convention on International Interests in Mobile Equipment (Cape Town) (co-sponsored by ICAO);
  - 2001 Protocol to the Convention on International Interests in Mobile Equipment on Matters specific to Aircraft Equipment (Cape Town) (co-sponsored by ICAO);
  - 2007 Luxembourg Protocol to the Convention on International Interests in Mobile Equipment on Matters specific to Railway Rolling Stock (co-sponsored by OTIF);
  - 2012 Protocol to the Convention on International Interests in Mobile Equipment on Matters specific to Space Assets (Berlin);
  - 2019 Protocol to the Convention on International Interests in Mobile Equipment on Matters specific to Mining, agricultural and Construction Equipment (Pretoria).
- 2002 Model Franchise Disclosure Law;
- 2008 UNIDROIT Model Law on Leasing;

Appendix 2. Instruments Adopted or Prepared by UNIDROIT

- 2009 UNIDROIT Convention on Substantive Rules for Intermediated Securities (Geneva);
- 2011 UNESCO–UNIDROIT Model Provisions on State Ownership of Undiscovered Cultural Objects.

In addition, UNIDROIT has published:

- UNIDROIT Principles of International Commercial Contracts (1994; 2nd ed. 2004; 3rd ed. 2010; 4th ed. 2016) (UNIDROIT Publications);
- Model Clauses for the Use of the UNIDROIT Principles of International Commercial Contracts (2013);
- Guide to International Master Franchise Arrangements (1998, 2nd ed. 2007) (UNIDROIT Publications);
- ALI / UNIDROIT Principles of Transnational Civil Procedure (2004) (Cambridge University Press, 2006);
- UNIDROIT/FAO/IFAD Legal Guide on Contract Farming (UNIDROIT/FAO/IFAD, 2015);
- Principles on the Operation of Close-Out Netting Provisions (2013);
- Official Commentary on the UNIDROIT Convention on Substantive Rules for Intermediated Securities (H. Kanda, C. Mooney, L. Thévenoz, S. Béraud. Assisted by T. Keijser – Oxford University Press, 2012);
- Official Commentary to the Convention on International Interests in Mobile Equipment and Protocol thereto on Matters Specific to Aircraft Equipment (R. Goode) (1st ed. 2002; 2nd ed. 2008; 3rd ed. 2013; 4th ed. 2019, 5th ed.2022); electronic version of the 5th ed. (2023) (UNIDROIT Publications);
- Official Commentary to the Convention on International Interest in Mobile Equipment and Luxembourg Protocol thereto on Matters Specific to Railway Rolling Stock (R. Goode) (1st ed. 2008; 2nd ed. 2014) (UNIDROIT Publications);
- Official Commentary to the Convention on International Interests in Mobile Equipment and Protocol thereto on Matters Specific to Space Assets (R. Goode) (2013) (UNIDROIT Publications);
- Official Commentary to the Convention on International Interests in Mobile Equipment and Protocol thereto on Matters Specific to Mining, Agricultural and Construction Equipment (R. Goode) (2021) (UNIDROIT Publications).

By reason of its expertise with respect to the international unification of law, UNIDROIT's work has also served as the basis for a number of international instruments adopted under the auspices of other international organisations. In these cases it is commissioned by the other organisations to prepare comparative law studies and/or draft Conventions designed to serve as the basis for either the preparation or the finalisation of the international instruments by those organisations. This was the case in particular in the period up to 1991. Only the instruments in force are listed below:

- 1954 Convention for the Protection of Cultural Property in the Event of Armed Conflict (UNESCO);

- 1955 Benelux Treaty on Compulsory Insurance against Civil Liability in respect of Motor Vehicles (Council of Europe);
- 1955 European Convention on Establishment (Council of Europe);
- 1956 Convention on the Contract for the International Carriage of Goods by Road (CMR) (UN/ECE);
- 1958 Hague Convention concerning the Recognition and Enforcement of Decisions relating to Maintenance Obligations towards Children (HCCH);
- 1959 European Convention on Compulsory Insurance against Civil Liability in respect of Motor Vehicles (Council of Europe);
- 1961 International Convention for the Protection of Performers, Producers of Phonograms and Broadcasting Organizations (ILO/UNESCO/WIPO);
- 1962 European Convention on the Liability of Hotel-keepers concerning the Property of their Guests (Council of Europe);
- Protocol No. 1 concerning the Rights in rem in Inland Navigation Vessels and Protocol No. 2 concerning Attachment and Forced Sale of Inland Navigation Vessels annexed to the 1965 Convention on the Registration of Inland Navigation Vessels (UN/ECE);
- 1973 Convention on the Contract for the International Carriage of Passengers and Luggage by Road (CVR) (UN/ECE).

Appendix 2. Instruments Adopted or Prepared by UNIDROIT

Appendix 3. UNIDROIT Publications

Uniform Law Review/*Revue de droit uniforme* (New Series)
Revue de droit uniforme /Uniform Law Review (Old Series)
Unification of Law – Yearbook
Uniform Law Cases

UNIFORM LAW REVIEW/*REVUE DE DROIT UNIFORME* (NEW SERIES)

The **Uniform Law Review/Revue de droit uniforme** is a bilingual (English/French) periodical which appears at quarterly intervals. It is the continuation of the publications **Unification of Law** (1948–1972) and the **Revue de droit uniforme/ Uniform Law Review** (old series) (1973–1995). In 1995 the Secretariat of the Institute felt that the time had come to modernize the Review and the new publication was launched in 1996 on the occasion of the 70th anniversary of the foundation of UNIDROIT. While UNIDROIT and its activities continue to be given prominence, the Review has also become a forum for debate on new developments in uniform private law as well as in legal harmonization and integration, whether worldwide or regional, and whether or not emanating from institutions whose primary function is to legislate. As from 2013 the Uniform Law Review is published by Oxford University Press.

REVUE DE DROIT UNIFORME/UNIFORM LAW REVIEW – (OLD SERIES)

The *Revue de droit uniforme*/Uniform Law Review (Old Series) appeared twice yearly from 1973 to 1995. It comprised a collection of materials on the continuing progress achieved in the field of the unification of law, in particular, it published the initial comparative law studies prepared for the projects undertaken by UNIDROIT, the drafts finalized by the committees and explanatory reports, periodical reports on the progress realized in the field of uniform law by other international and regional organizations, texts of uniform laws, conventions and other instruments adopted at international level, an updated bibliography and a regular selection of case law of various countries illustrating their application of uniform law texts.

UNIFICATION DU DROIT ANNUAIRE/UNIFICATION OF LAW YEARBOOK (1957–1972)

The Uniform Law Review was preceded by a publication with the title 'Unification of Law Yearbook' which the organization began to publish a few years after the establishment of UNIDROIT as an autonomous organization in 1940. It reflected the conviction that the dissemination of the work of organizations involved in the unification of law was the key to making instruments better known in order to ensure both their adoption and application by the greatest number of States or professional groups. The Yearbook series deals with achievements in the field of the unification of law in the years 1956 to 1971. Each Yearbook contains a general survey of work for the unification of private law (a survey of the work of UNIDROIT; texts of international conventions and drafts of international conventions based on the work of UNIDROIT; a survey of the achievements of unification; international conventions adopted and draft conventions; a bibliography on the unification of law).

UNIFICATION OF LAW – *UNIFICATION DU DROIT* (1948–1956) IN 4 VOLUMES

Before the organization decided to publish a Yearbook, it published four volumes which summarized achievements until that point in time:

> Vol. I contains a general survey of work for the unification of private law 1926–1946
> Vol. II contains the Actes du Congrès international de droit privé tenu à Rome en juillet 1950 [French version only]
> Vol. III contains a general survey of work for the unification of private law 1947–1952, and
> Vol. IV contains a general survey of work for the unification of private law 1953– 195.

UNIFORM LAW CASES – JURISPRUDENCE DE DROIT UNIFORME (1959–1971)

Between 1959 and 1971 the section of the Yearbook which up until 1958 had dealt with case law was published separately in the series *Jurisprudence de droit uniforme* – Uniform Law Cases. It comprised a selection of case law of various countries illustrating their application and interpretation of uniform law texts.

Acts and Proceedings of Diplomatic Conferences for the Adoption of UNIDROIT Conventions

The Acts and Proceedings of Diplomatic Conferences contain the basic working materials, papers submitted by participating delegations to the various organs of the Conference, the summary records of the sessions of the various committees and the texts adopted.

ACTS AND PROCEEDINGS OF THE DIPLOMATIC CONFERENCE TO ADOPT A MOBILE EQUIPMENT CONVENTION AND AN AIRCRAFT PROTOCOL, NOVEMBER 2001, CAPE TOWN

This volume reproduces the basic Conference working materials, that is the texts submitted to the Conference for adoption, in particular the draft Convention, the working papers submitted to the different organs of the Conference, the summary records of all sessions of both the Conference Plenum and the Committee of the Whole, as well as the texts and instruments adopted by the Conference.

DIPLOMATIC CONFERENCE FOR THE ADOPTION OF THE DRAFT UNIDROIT CONVENTION ON THE INTERNATIONAL RETURN OF STOLEN OR ILLEGALLY EXPORTED CULTURAL OBJECTS, ROME, 7 TO 24 JUNE 1995 – ACTS AND PROCEEDINGS

This volume reproduces the basic Conference working materials, that is the texts submitted to the Conference for adoption, in particular, the draft Convention together with its explanatory report, the working papers submitted to the different organs of the Conference, the summary records of all sessions of both the Conference Plenum and the Committee of the Whole, as well as the texts and instruments adopted by the Conference (*Roma, Presidenza del Consiglio dei Ministri, Dipartimento per l'Informazione e l'Editoria*, 1996).

ACTS AND PROCEEDINGS OF THE DIPLOMATIC CONFERENCE FOR THE ADOPTION OF THE DRAFT UNIDROIT CONVENTIONS ON INTERNATIONAL FACTORING AND INTERNATIONAL FINANCIAL LEASING, OTTAWA, 9–28 MAY 1988 (2 VOLUMES)

Volume I reproduces all the basic Conference working materials, that is the texts submitted to the Conference for adoption, in particular, the two draft Conventions together with their explanatory reports, and the working papers and reports submitted to the different organs of the Conference, as well as the texts and instruments adopted by the Conference.
Volume II contains the summary records of all sessions of both the Conference Plenum and the Committee of the Whole as well as a complete list of all the papers issued in connection with the Conference (Rome, UNIDROIT, 1991– 1992).

DIPLOMATIC CONFERENCE FOR THE ADOPTION OF THE UNIDROIT DRAFT CONVENTION ON AGENCY IN THE INTERNATIONAL SALE OF GOODS, GENEVA 31 JANUARY–17 FEBRUARY 1983 – ACTS AND PROCEEDINGS

This volume reproduces the basic Conference working materials, that is the texts submitted to the Conference for adoption, in particular, the draft Convention together with its explanatory report, the working papers submitted to the different organs of the Conference, the summary records of all sessions of both the Conference Plenum and the Committee of the Whole, as well as the texts and instruments adopted by the Conference. These Acts were published as Volume 1983/I– II of the Uniform Law Review.

OFFICIAL COMMENTARY ON THE CONVENTION ON INTERNATIONAL INTERESTS IN MOBILE EQUIPMENT AND THE PROTOCOL THERETO ON MATTERS SPECIFIC TO AIRCRAFT EQUIPMENT, BY PROFESSOR SIR ROY GOODE (2002; 2ND ED. 2008, 3RD ED. 2013, 4TH ED. 2019, 5TH ED. 2022; 5TH ED. ELECTRONIC VERSION 2023)

This authoritative guide, after a brief historical introduction, provides an Overview of the Convention and Protocol followed by a detailed analysis of each of the ninety-nine Articles comprising the two instruments, together with illustrative examples. Also incorporated in this volume are Annexes, which include the Final Act of the Diplomatic Conference, a Table of Concordance with the Consolidated Text prepared as a working tool by the UNIDROIT and ICAO Secretariats, a matrix of the declarations permitted by the two instruments, details of the key events and documents leading up to their conclusion and an index.

Appendix 3. UNIDROIT Publications

As Chairman of the UNIDROIT Study Group that initiated this project, Rapporteur to the three Joint Sessions of the UNIDROIT Committee of Governmental Experts and the ICAO Legal Sub-Committee, and Chairman of the Drafting Committee at the Diplomatic Conference, Professor Sir Roy Goode was uniquely qualified to fulfil the mandate given to him by the Diplomatic Conference to prepare an Official Commentary on the Convention and Aircraft Equipment Protocol.

OFFICIAL COMMENTARY ON THE CONVENTION ON INTERNATIONAL INTERESTS IN MOBILE EQUIPMENT AND PROTOCOL THERETO ON MATTERS SPECIFIC TO MINING, AGRICULTURAL AND CONSTRUCTION EQUIPMENT, BY PROFESSOR SIR ROY GOODE (2021)

The Pretoria Official Commentary consists of narrative text, annotations to the two instruments containing 77 illustrative examples and several appendices, together running to some 790 pages. It provides a comprehensive and authoritative guide which is indispensable for all manufacturers, financiers, lessors and their legal advisors involved in transactions relating to MAC equipment.

OFFICIAL COMMENTARY ON THE CONVENTION ON INTERNATIONAL INTERESTS IN MOBILE EQUIPMENT AND LUXEMBOURG PROTOCOL THERETO ON MATTERS SPECIFIC TO RAILWAY ROLLING STOCK, BY PROFESSOR SIR ROY GOODE (2007, 2ND ED. 2014)

This authoritative guide, after a brief historical introduction, provides an Overview of the Convention and Protocol followed by a detailed analysis of each of the ninety-six Articles comprising the two instruments. Also incorporated in this volume are Annexes, which include the Final Act of the Diplomatic Conference, a matrix of the declarations permitted by the two instruments, details of the key events and documents leading up to their conclusion and an index.

OFFICIAL COMMENTARY ON THE CONVENTION ON INTERNATIONAL INTERESTS IN MOBILE EQUIPMENT AND THE PROTOCOL THERETO ON MATTERS SPECIFIC TO SPACE ASSETS, BY PROFESSOR SIR ROY GOODE (2013)

This Official Commentary provides a detailed analysis of the Convention and Space Protocol and benefits not only from the input of experts from the space industry but also from ideas exchanged with experts from the aviation industry, in the light of their experience, on matters common to all three categories of equipment covered by the Convention.

Official Commentary on the Convention on International Interests in Mobile Equipment and the Protocol thereto on Matters Specific to Mining, Agricultural and Construction Equipment, by Professor Sir Roy Goode (2021).

This Official Commentary provides a detailed analysis of the Convention and MAC Protocol and benefits from the input of experts from the mining, agricultural and construction industries. It consists of narrative text, annotations to the two instruments containing 77 illustrative examples and several appendices, including the Final Act of the Diplomatic Conference, a matrix of the declarations permitted by the two instruments, details of the key events and documents leading up to their conclusion and an index, together running to some 790 pages.

MODEL FRANCHISE DISCLOSURE LAW (2004)

The Model Franchise Disclosure Law was adopted in 2002 and is the first model law produced by UNIDROIT. It is a disclosure law, and consequently is limited to regulating disclosure and does not regulate the relations between the parties to a franchise agreement. It is composed of a Preamble and the ten articles of the Model Law itself. It includes a detailed provision on the disclosure requirements themselves (Art. 6), but also indicates applicable exceptions (Art. 5) and remedies (Art. 9). It is accompanied by an Explanatory Report illustrating the provisions.

MODEL LAW ON LEASING (2008)

The text of the Model Law on Leasing was first published in the Uniform Law Review 2009 at page 648 (in English) and 649 (French). The Official Commentary followed in the Uniform Law Review 2010 at page 548 (in English) and 549 (in French). The two language versions are published face to face.

UNIDROIT PRINCIPLES OF INTERNATIONAL COMMERCIAL CONTRACTS 4TH ED. (2016)

UNIDROIT PRINCIPLES OF INTERNATIONAL COMMERCIAL CONTRACTS 3RD ED.(2010)

UNIDROIT PRINCIPLES OF INTERNATIONAL COMMERCIAL CONTRACTS 2ND ED.(2004)

UNIDROIT PRINCIPLES OF INTERNATIONAL COMMERCIAL CONTRACTS 1ST ED. (1994)

The UNIDROIT Principles of International Commercial Contracts 1994 are composed of a Preamble and 119 articles divided into seven chapters, namely 'General Provisions' (Chapter 1); 'Formation' (Chapter 2); 'Validity' (Chapter 3); 'Interpretation' (Chapter 4); 'Content' (Chapter 5); 'Performance' (Chapter 6) and 'Non-Performance' (Chapter 7). Chapter 6 has two sections dealing with 'Performance in General' and 'Hardship' respectively, while Chapter 7 has four sections, namely 'Non-Performance in General', 'Right to Performance', 'Termination', and 'Damages'. The 'black-letter rules' are accompanied by detailed comments, including illustrations, which form an integral part of the Principles.

The integral version of the UNIDROIT Principles of International Commercial Contracts 1994 exists in five official language versions – English, French, German, Italian and Spanish – as well as in Arabic, Chinese, Czech, Dutch, Hungarian, Portuguese, Russian, Slovak and Vietnamese.

At its annual session in 2004 the Governing Council of UNIDROIT unanimously adopted the new edition of the UNIDROIT Principles of International Commercial Contracts. As compared to the 1994 edition, UNIDROIT Principles 2004 contains five new sections and chapters (Authority of Agents; Third Party Rights; Set-off; Assignment of Rights, Transfer of Obligations and Assignment of Contracts; Limitation Periods) as well as an expanded Preamble and new provisions on Inconsistent

Behaviour and Release by Agreement. Moreover, wherever appropriate the 1994 edition of the Principles was adapted to meet the needs of electronic contracting.

In the third, 2010, edition, Chapter 3 has been divided into sections, the existing provisions being divided into Section 1 (General Provisions) and Section 2 (Defects of consent). Article 3.17(1) has become Article 3.2.14, Article 3.17(2) has become Article 3.2.15 and Article 3.19 has been moved and has become Article 3.1.4. A new Section 3 (Illegality) has been added. A new Section 3 (Conditions) has been added to Chapter 5, and the article on Restitution in Chapter 7 (Article 7.3.6) has been replaced by two articles: Article 7.3.6 on Restitution with respect to contracts to be performed at one time and 7.3.7 on Restitution with respect to contracts to be performed over a period of time. A new Chapter 11 has been added on the Plurality of Obligors and of Obligees.

For the fourth, 2016, edition, to take the requirements of long-term contracts into consideration, the content of the 2010 edition was altered only marginally: only six provisions having been amended (the Preamble and Articles 1.11, 2.1.14, 5.1.7, 5.1.8, and 7.3.7). The majority of alterations were made to the Comments, in particular on the Preamble (amendments to Comment 2) and Articles 1.11 (addition of a new Comment 3), 2.1.14 (amendments to Comments 1–3 and the addition of a new Comment 4), 2.1.15 (amendments to Comment 2 and addition of a new Comment 3), 4.3 (amendments to Comment 3 (which has become Comment 4) and addition of a new Comment 3), 4.8 (amendments to Comments 1–3), 5.1.3 (amendments to the Comment (which has become Comment 1) and addition of a new Comment 2), 5.1.4 (addition of a new Comment 3), 5.1.7 (amendments to Comments 2–3), 5.1.8 (amendments to the Comment (which has become Comment 1) and addition of a new Comment 2), 7.1.7 (addition of a new Comment 5), 7.3.5 (amendments to Comment 3 and addition of a new Comment 4), 7.3.6 (amendments to Comment 1), and 7.3.7 (amendments to Comments 1–2).

GUIDE TO INTERNATIONAL MASTER FRANCHISE ARRANGEMENTS (1998; 2ND ED. 2007)

The UNIDROIT Guide to International Master Franchise Arrangements offers a comprehensive examination of the whole life of master franchise arrangements, from the negotiation and drafting of the master franchise agreement itself and other associated agreements to the end of the relationship and its effects. It deals principally with the positions of the parties directly involved, i.e., the franchisor and the subfranchisor, but, in instances where it is considered to be of particular importance, the positions of others affected, such as sub-franchisees, are covered (Rome, UNIDROIT, 1998; second edition 2007).

ELI-UNIDROIT MODEL EUROPEAN RULES OF CIVIL PROCEDURE

EUROPEAN LAW INSTITUTE (ELI) AND INTERNATIONAL INSTITUTE FOR THE UNIFICATION OF PRIVATE LAW (UNIDROIT) OXFORD UNIVERSITY PRESS, OXFORD, 2021

The Model Rules cover a broad range of issues concerning the commencement, structure, conduct and conclusion of civil proceedings, including a section on appeals and on collective redress. They are aimed at offering detailed guidance for further development of civil procedure in Europe and beyond. In August 2021, the integral version in English of the Model Rules was published by Oxford University Press, as part of the ELI publication series. The publication is open access.

The black-letter rules in French were drafted in 2020 by the French Task Force of the Structure Group in cooperation with the Final Drafting Team of the Structure Group, while the translation of the comments was finalised by the UNIDROIT Secretariat. Unofficial translations of the Model Rules are in preparation in several languages (among which Chinese, Farsi, German, Spanish, and Ukrainian).

UNIDROIT/FAO/IFAD LEGAL GUIDE ON CONTRACT FARMING ROME, UNIDROIT, 2015

The first joint venture with the Food and Agriculture Organization of the United Nations (FAO) and the International Fund for Agricultural Development (IFAD), the Guide is intended to offer a thorough analysis of substantive law issues that are involved in contract farming, identifying problem areas and possible solutions in light of trade usages and legislation.

UNIDROIT/IFAD LEGAL GUIDE ON AGRICULTURAL LAND INVESTMENT CONTRACTS, ROME, UNIDROIT 2021

The ALIC Legal Guide discusses how to identify and involve equitably all relevant parties and stakeholders in agricultural land investment and how to structure the resulting contracts. The ALIC Legal Guide demonstrates how international private law instruments can be used to implement a number of the UN Sustainable Development Goals. By building upon the UNIDROIT Principles of International Commercial Contracts (UPICC), the ALIC Legal Guide provides guidance on the rights and socio-environmental contractual obligations of the parties. It also provides detailed guidance on how to conduct: consultations based on the FPIC principle (Free, Prior, and Informed Consent), due diligence, impact assessments, the disclosure of non-financial information, cases of contractual non-performance, grievance mechanisms and dispute resolution procedures for both contracting parties, as well as for third-party beneficiaries.

Acts and Proceedings of UNIDROIT Congresses

One way of achieving the statutory aims of UNIDROIT is the organization of congresses or colloquies on topics related to the unification of law. Various events of this type have been organized over the years (in 1950, 1976, 1987, 1996 and 2002) and the proceedings have been published either as a special issue of the Review or as a separate publication.

WORLDWIDE HARMONISATION OF PRIVATE LAW AND REGIONAL ECONOMIC INTEGRATION, ROME, 27–28 SEPTEMBER 2002. ACTS OF THE CONGRESS TO CELEBRATE THE 75TH ANNIVERSARY OF THE FOUNDING OF THE INTERNATIONAL INSTITUTE FOR THE UNIFICATION OF PRIVATE LAW (UNIDROIT).

This volume contains reports in English and French on:

> Modernization and harmonization of contract law: objectives, methods and scope.
> The sale of goods: do regions matter?

Appendix 3. UNIDROIT Publications

Unificatory and de-unificatory forces in the law of the carriage of goods: where do we go from here?

Harmonized modernization of the law governing secured transactions: general- –sectorial.

Global-regional international civil procedure and transnational Civil procedure: the impact of regional economic integration.

Private law beyond markets for goods and services: the example of cultural objects and

the reports presented in a Special forum – economic analysis and harmonized modernization of private law (published in the special issue of the Uniform Law Review/*Revue de droit uniforme*, 2003, Issue 1/2).

INTERNATIONAL UNIFORM LAW IN PRACTICE /*LE DROIT UNIFORME INTERNATIONAL DANS LA PRATIQUE*

Acts and Proceedings of the 3rd Congress on Private Law held by the International Institute for the Unification of Private Law (UNIDROIT), Rome 7–10 September 1987.

This volume contains reports in English or French on:

Uniform law and its introduction into national law.
Uniform law and its application by judges and arbitrators.
Uniform law and its impact on business circles.
(Rome, International Institute for the Unification of Private Law (UNIDROIT), 1988).

NEW DIRECTIONS IN INTERNATIONAL TRADE LAW

Acts and Proceedings of the 2nd Congress on Private Law held by the International Institute for the Unification of Private Law (UNIDROIT), Rome, 9–15 September 1976 (two volumes).

These two volumes contain reports in English or French on:

The law of international trade: a new task for national legislators or a new '*lex mercatoria*'?
The autonomy of the contracting parties in international trade relations.
The relevance of course of dealing, usages and customs in the interpretation of international contracts of adhesion and the protection of the weaker party in international trade relations.
The international unification and harmonization of the law regarding multinational companies.
The State as a party to contracts concerning concessions or investments with foreign private companies.
Anti-trust rules and concentration between firms on an international scale.
(Dobbs Ferry, NY, Oceana Publications, Inc., 1977).

ACTES DU CONGRÈS INTERNATIONAL DE DROIT PRIVÉ TENU À ROME EN JUILLET 1950

The proceedings of this Congress, in French only, were published as Volume II of the series *Unification du droit.*

LOS PRINCIPIOS DE UNIDROIT: ¿ UN DERECHO COMÚN DE LOS CONTRATOS PARA LAS AMÉRICAS?/THE UNIDROIT PRINCIPLES: A COMMON LAW OF CONTRACTS FOR THE AMERICAS?

(Actas/Acts – Congreso Interamericano/Inter-American Congress – *Hacia un nuevo régimen para la contractación internacional: los Principios de UNIDROIT sobre los contratos comerciales internacionales*/A new approach to international commercial relations: the UNIDROIT Principles of international Commercial Contracts, Valencia, Venezuela –6–9 *Noviembre*/November 1996) (Rome, International Institute for the Unification of Private Law (UNIDROIT), 1998).

Other Publications

EPPUR SI MUOVE: THE AGE OF UNIFORM LAW. ESSAYS IN HONOUR OF MICHAEL JOACHIM BONELL TO CELEBRATE HIS 70TH BIRTHDAY

The Essays in honour of Professor Michael Joachim Bonell, a long-time collaborator and consultant to UNIDROIT as well as the chief promotor and coordinator of the Principles of International Commercial Contracts comprise some 122 articles by 125 authors. The articles cover: Personal Reminiscences; Legal Theory; Comparative Law, Transnational Law and Uniform Law in General; Private International Law; European Law; Contract Law; International Contract Law; UNIDROIT Principles of International Commercial Contracts; Sales and Other Types of Contract; Company, Banking, Insolvency and Intellectual Property Law; Capital Markets; Property Law; Cultural Property; Succession; Arbitration and ADR; and Civil Procedure Law.

Appendix 3. UNIDROIT Publications

Appendix 4. Depository Libraries for UNIDROIT Documentation

In order to make the documents issued by UNIDROIT more readily available in its member States, some member States have designated libraries to which UNIDROIT documentation is sent regularly.

The following are Depository Libraries for UNIDROIT documentation:

Argentina	Corte Suprema de Justicia de la Nación, Secretaría de Investigación de Derecho comparado, Buenos Aires
Australia	National Library of Australia
Austria	Universität Wien, Universitäts Bibliothek, Fachbereichsbibliothek Rechtswissenschaften
Belgium	Ministry of Justice
Bolivia	Biblioteca Central de la Cancillería de la República
Brazil	Serviço de Biblioteca e documentação – SBD, Universidad de São Paulo, Faculdade de Direito
Bulgaria	Bulgarian National Library 'St. Cyrill and St. Methodius'
Canada	Nahum Gelber Law Library, McGill University
	University of British Columbia Law Library
Chile	Diplomatic Academy of the Republic of Chile
Colombia	Biblioteca Luis Angel Arango
Czech Republic	Library of the International Law Department, Ministry of Industry and Trade, (Ministerstvo prumyslu a obchodu) Prague
	Charles University in Prague
Egypt	Documentation Center, General Directorate of International and Cultural Co-operation, Ministry of Justice, Cairo
Estonia	National Library of Estonia
Finland	Library of Parliament (Eduskunnan Kurjasto)
France	Bibliothèque Inter-universitaire Cujas

Appendix 4. Depository Libraries for UNIDROIT Documentation

Germany	Staatsbibliothek zu Berlin, Abteilung Amtsdruckschriften und Internationaler Amtlicher Schriftentausch
Greece	Library of the Hellenic Institute of International and Foreign Law, Athens
Holy See	Biblioteca della Facoltà di Giurisprudenza, Libera Università Maria Ss. Assunta, Rome
Hungary	Library of the Hungarian Parliament, Budapest
India	Library of the Indian Society of International Law, New Delhi
Indonesia	Departemen Luar Negeri (Directorate for Economic, Social and Cultural Treaties Affairs, Directorate General of Legal and Treaties Affairs, Ministry of Foreign Affairs), Jakarta
Iran (the Islamic Republic of	Institute of Comparative Law: Faculty of Law and Political Science of the University of Tehran
Ireland	National Library of Ireland, Dublin
Japan	Ministry of Justice Library (Branch of National Diet Library), Tokyo
Latvia	Department of European and International Law, Ministry of Justice of the Republic of Latvia
Luxembourg	Bibliothèque Nationale, Luxembourg
	Centre Universitaire de Luxembourg
Malta	Library Services, University of Malta
Mexico	Instituto de Investigaciones Jurídicas, Universidad Nacional Autónoma de México
	Academia Mexicana de Derecho Internacional Privado y Comparado, México City
	Biblioteca Loyola, Universidad Iberoamericana Tijuana
Netherlands	Library of the Ministry of Justice
Norway	Det juridiske fakultetsbibliotek, Universiteitsbiblioteket i Oslo
Paraguay	Facultad de Derecho y Ciencias Sociales de la Universidad Nacional de Asunción
People's Republic of China	Trade Policy Library, Department of Treaty and Law, Ministry of Foreign Trade and Economic Cooperation (MOFCOM)
Poland	Biblioteka Sejmowa

Portugal	Serviço de Biblioteca e Documentação Diplomática do Ministério dos Negócios Estrangeiros – Instituto Diplomático
	Gabinete de Documentação e Direito Comparado, Procuradoria Geral da República
Republic of Korea	Library of the Institute for Foreign Affairs and National Security (IFANS), Seoul
Romania	Biblioteca Nationala, Serviciul Primiri, Bucuresti
Russian Federation	Library of the Russian Foreign Trade Academy, Moscow
Serbia	Library of the Institute of Comparative Law
Slovakia	Právnická faculta Trnavskej Univerzity, Trnava
Slovenia	Library of the Faculty of Law, University of Maribor
South Africa	Library of the Department of Justice, Directorate: Internal Affairs, Pretoria
	University of Johannesburg
Spain	Universidad San Pablo CEU, Madrid
Sweden	Library of the Swedish Parliament (Sveriges Riksdag)
Switzerland	Library of the Swiss Institute of Comparative Law
Turkey	Library, Banca ve Ticaret Hukuku Arastirma Enstitüsü (The Research Institute of Banking and Commercial Law), Hukuk Fakültesi, Ankara
United Kingdom	Library of the Institute of Advanced Legal Studies, London
United States of America	Arthur W. Diamond Law Library Columbia University in the City of New York
	Underwood Law Library, Dedman School of Law, Southern Methodist University, Dallas
Uruguay	Biblioteca, Facultad de Derecho de la Universidad de la República, Montevideo

Appendix 4. Depository Libraries for UNIDROIT Documentation

Appendix 5. The UNIDROIT Web Site

The UNIDROIT Internet site was created in 1996, revamped in 2014 and re-elaborated in 2022 to take recent developments in software technology into consideration: <www.unidroit.org>.

The UNIDROIT Web site contains, in both English and French, information on the organization and its current and past projects, thc tcxt of its adopted texts and of the documents that form the background to these texts, publications and other information relevant to the organization and its work. The website is continuously developing, with new categories of materials being added daily.

Appendix 5. The UNIDROIT Web Site

Selected Bibliography

The *Uniform Law Review* published a *Uniform Law Bibliography* which included references not only to instruments prepared by UNIDROIT but also to other instruments of uniform private law and related comparative law issues. In view of the ever-greater accessibility of bibliographical information on the Internet, this section of the Uniform Law Review was discontinued. With the exception of the general bibliography on the Institute, the following bibliography includes only bibliographical references to UNIDROIT projects and instruments published in 2000 or thereafter. References until 2017 are taken from the Uniform Law Bibliography that was published in the Uniform Law Review.

General Bibliography on the Institute

In recent years, only a few works have been written about UNIDROIT in general, most articles concentrating on one or other subject, or at the most dealing with a couple at the same time. The general articles written on UNIDROIT include:

Całus, A. 'Miþdzynarodowy Instytut Unifikacji Prawa Prywatnego'. *Kwartalnik Prawa Prywatnego* VIII (1999): 1–68.

Cavarretta. L'Istituto internazionale per l'unificazione del diritto privato. Messina, 1929.

Chialvo. L'Istituto internazionale per l'unificazione del diritto privato. Roma, 1931.

Estrella Faria, J.A. 'Future Directions of Legal Harmonisation and Law Reform: Stormy Seas or Prosperous Voyage?' *Uniform Law Review* (2009): 5–34.

Gabriel, H.D. 'The Advantages of Soft Law in International Commercial Law: The Role of UNIDROIT, UNCITRAL and The Hague Conference'. *Symposium [on] ruling the world* (2009): 655–672.

Kronke, H. 'The scope of Party Autonomy in Recent UNIDROIT Instruments and the Conflict of Laws in the Mercosur and the European Union'. *Liber amicorum en homenaje al profesor Dr Didier Opertti Badán* (2005): 289–302.

Kronke, H. 'A Bridge Out of the Fortress: UNIDROIT's Work on Global Modernisation of Commercial Law and its Relevance for Europe'. *Zeitschrift für europäisches Privatrecht* 16 (2008): 1–5.

Kronke, H. 'Transnationales Handelsrecht in der Reifeprüfung: Die UNIDROIT–Arbeiten 1998–2008': Referat im Rahmen der Vortragsreihe 'Rechtsfragen der Europäischen Integration' Bonn, den 02.02.2009, Bonn, Zentrum für Europ. Wirtschaftsrecht, 2009, A. Heldrich, & K.J. Hopt 20 (*Vorträge und Berichte / Zentrum für Europäisches Wirtschaftsrecht*, 174).

Monaco, R. 'Istituto internazionale per l'unificazione del diritto privato (UNIDROIT)'. *Enc. giur* XVIII. Roma, 1988.

Rabel, E. 'Zwei Rechtsinstitute für die internationalen privatrechtlichen Beziehungen'. *Juristische Wochenschrift* (1932): 2225.

Rodinò, W. 'UNIDROIT', *Il Digesto*. IV Edizione, Aggiornamento. Torino: UTET, 2000.

Rudolf, K. 'Organizations Active in the Unification of Private Law: International Institute for the Unification of Private Law (UNIDROIT)'. *Introduction to Transnational Legal Transactions*. New York: Dobbs Ferry, 1995.

Stanford, M.J. 'Istituto Internazionale per l'Unificazione del Diritto Privato (UNIDROIT)'. *Enciclopedia giuridica, aggiornamento* (2007): 1–2.

Veigel, J. 'Die funktionale Methode bei der Rechtsvergleichung'. *Juridica international* 2021, 30 (2021): 71–80.

Winship, P. 'Introduction to Harmonization of Private Law'. *Introduction to Transnational Legal Transactions.* New York: Dobbs Ferry, 1995.

Zanobetti Pagnetti, A. 'UNIDROIT's Recent Work: An Appraisal'. *Yearbook of Private International Law*, 2012, 13 (2011), 345–365.

UNIDROIT Principles of International Commercial Contracts

In addition to bibliographical references to books and articles, a selection of the most recent of which is given below, the UNILEX database contains reports on arbitral awards and cases decided by national courts relating to the Principles (*see* <www.unilex.info>).

Araújo, N. de. 'A cláusula de Hardship nos contratos internacionais e a sua regulamentação nos princípios para os contratos comerciais internacionais do UNIDROIT'. In *Contratos internacionais: autonomia da vontade, Mercosul e convenções internacionais.*, 3. ed., rev. y ampliada, Rio de Janeiro et al.: Renovar, 2006.

Audit, B. 'Le choix des Principes d'UNIDROIT comme loi du contrat et le droit international privé'. *Liber amicorum: mélanges en l'honneur de Camille Jauffret-Spinosi*, 2013, pp. 13–29.

Belohlávek, A.J. 'Scope of jurisdiction of tribunals and internatioonal authorities in interpretation of international law'. *International Justice and International Enforcement*. The Hague: 23–73.

Basedow, J. 'Depositivierungstendenzen in der Rechtsprechung zum Internationalen Einheitsrecht'. *50 Jahre Bundesgerichtshof. Festgabe aus der Wissenschaft*, A. Heldrich, & K.J. Hopt (Hrsg.) Band II, *Handels- und Wirtschaftsrecht, Europäisches und Internationales Recht*. München: Beck, 2000.

Baumann, A. 'Regeln der Auslegung internationaler Handelsgeschäfte: eine vergleichende Untersuchung der UNIDROIT Principles, der Principles of European Contract Law, des Uniform Commercial Code und des deutschen Rechts', 1. Aufl. – Göttingen: V & R Unipress, 2004, 216 *(Schriften zum internationalen Privatrecht und zur Rechtsvergleichung*; 19).

Bennett, H. 'Agency in the Principles of European Contract Law and the UNIDROIT Principles of International Commercial Contracts (2004)'. *Uniform Law Review* 11 (2006): 771–793.

Ben-Oliel, R. 'The UNIDROIT Principles of International Commercial Contracts: A comment',. in: *The Principles of UNIDROIT and Modern National Codifications*, edited by A.M. Rabello. Jerusalem: Harry and Michael Sacher Institute for Legislative Research and Comparative Law, Faculty of Law, The Hebrew University of Jerusalem, 2001.

Berger, K.P. 'The Relationship between the UNIDROIT Principles of International Commercial Contracts and the New Lex Mercatoria'.*International Uniform Law Conventions, Lex Mercatoria and UNIDROIT Principles.* Symposium held at Verona University (Italy), Faculty of Law, 4–6 November 1999. *Uniform Law Review* (2000): 152–170.

Berger, K.P. 'The role of the UNIDROIT Principles of International Commercial Contracts in international contract practice: the UNIDROIT Model Clauses'. *Uniform Law Review*, 19 (2014), pp. 519–541.

Bernardini, P. 'UNIDROIT Principles and international investment arbitration'. *Uniform Law Review*, 19 (2014), pp. 561–569.

Böckstiegel, K.-H. 'The Application of the UNIDROIT Principles to Contracts Involving States or Intergovernmental Organizations'. *UNIDROIT Principles of International Contracts. Reflections on Their Use in International Arbitration, ICC International Court of Arbitration Bulletin* (2002): 51–55.

Boggiano, A. 'Elección ("kollisionsrechtlige Verweisung") de los Principios UNIDROIT como el derecho aplicable a los contratos internacionales. Propuesta de modificación estructural de los Principios UNIDROIT', edited by UNIDROIT, *Eppur si muove: The Age of Uniform Law. Essays in Honour of Michael Joachim Bonell to Celebrate His 70th Birthday*, Vol. 2 (2016), pp. 1197–1257.

Bonell, M.J. 'The UNIDROIT Principles and Transnational Law'. *Uniform Law Review* (2000): 199–218.

Bonell, M.J. 'UNIDROIT Principles of International Commercial Contracts and the United Nations Convention on Contracts for the International Sale of Goods – Alternatives or Complementary Instruments?'. *Business Law International* (2000): 89–98.

Bonell, M.J. 'The UNIDROIT Principles of International Commercial Contracts: The first 50 or so decisions'. *New Trends in International Trade Law. Contributions on the occasion of the 10th Anniversary of the International Trade Law Course.* Torino: G. Giappichelli Editore, 2000.

Bonell, M.J. & T. Monfeli. 'Rassegna giurisprudenziale sui Principi UNIDROIT dei Contratti Commerciali Internazionali'. *Diritto del Commercio Internazionale* 15 (2001): 169–210.

Bonell, M.J. 'A "Global" Arbitration Decided on the Basis of the UNIDROIT Principles: In re *Andersen Consulting Business Unit Member Firms v. Arthur Andersen Business Unit Member Firms and Andersen Worldwide Société Coopérative*'. *Arbitration International* 17 (2001): 249–261.

Bonell, M.J. 'A "Global" Arbitration Decided on the Basis of the UNIDROIT Principles. In re *Andersen Consulting Business Unit Member Firms v. Arthur Andersen Business Unit Member Firms and Andersen Worldwide Société Coopérative*'. *Aufbruch nach Europa. 75 Jahre Max-Planck-Institut für Privatrecht*, edited by J. Basedow, U. Drobnig & R. Ellger et al. Tübingen: Mohr Siebeck, 2001.

Selected Bibliography

Bonell, M.J. 'The UNIDROIT Principles and Transnational Law'. *The Practice of Transnational Law*, edited by K.P. Berger. The Hague: London, Kluwer Law International, 2001.

Bonell, M.J. 'The UNIDROIT Principles of International Commercial Contracts: Why? What? How?'. *The Principles of UNIDROIT and Modern National Codifications*, edited by A.M. Rabello. Jerusalem: Harry and Michael Sacher Institute for Legislative Research and Comparative Law, Faculty of Law, The Hebrew University of Jerusalem, 2001.

Bonell, M.J. 'Un arbitrato "globale" deciso sulla base dei Principi UNIDROIT'. *Diritto del Commercio Internazionale* 15 (2001): 211–236.

Bonell, M.J. 'The UNIDROIT Principles of International Commercial Contracts and the Harmonisation of International Sales Law'. *Foundations and Perspectives of International Trade Law*, edited by I. Fletcher, L. Mistelis & M. Cremona. London: Sweet & Maxwell, 2001.

Bonell, M.J. (ed.). *I Principi UNIDROIT nella pratica. Casistica e bibliografia riguardanti i Principi UNIDROIT dei contratti commerciali internazionali.* Milano: Giuffrè, 2002, XI–787 (Contratti & Commercio Internazionale).

Bonell, M.J. 'Les Principes d'UNIDROIT comme moyen d'interpréter et de compléter le droit international uniforme'. *Principes d'UNIDROIT relatifs aux contrats du commerce international. Réflexions sur leur utilisation dans l'arbitrage international, Bulletin de la Cour internationale d'arbitrage de la CCI* Supplément spécial (2002): 29–38.

Bonell, M.J. 'The UNIDROIT Principles as a Means of Interpreting and Supplementing International Uniform Law'. *UNIDROIT Principles of International Commercial Contracts. Reflections on Their Use in International Arbitration, ICC International Court of Arbitration Bulletin.* Special supplement (2002): 29–38.

Bonell, M.J. & Peleggi, R. (a cura di). 'Rassegna giurisprudenziale sui Principi UNIDROIT dei contratti commerciali internazionali'. *Diritto del Commercio Internazionale* 16 (2002): 443–461.

Bonell, M.J. (ed.). *The UNIDROIT Principles in Practice: Caselaw and Bibliography on the Principles of Commercial Contracts.* Ardsley, New York: Transnational Publishers, 2002.

Bonell, M.J. 'The UNIDROIT Principles as a Means of Interpreting and Supplementing Uniform Law International Arbitration Practice'. *DeCITA* 2 (2004): 86–100.

Bonell, M.J. 'UNIDROIT Principles 2004: A Further Step Towards a Global Contract Law'. *Uniform Commercial Code Law Journal* 37(1) (2004): 1, 49–148.

Bonell, M.J. 'An International Restatement of Contract Law: The UNIDROIT Principles of International Commercial Contracts', 3rd edn. Irvington, New York: Transnational Juris Publication, 2005, XIII-691.

Bonell, M.J. 'Perché non un Codice commerciale universale?' *Global law v. local law: problemi della globalizzazione giuridica: 17. Ponzanelli, G. – Amato, C. (eds), colloquio biennale Associazione italiana di diritto comparato*, Brescia, 12–14 *maggio* 2005, 2006.

Bonell, M.J. 'The UNIDROIT Principles in Practice: Caselaw and Bibliography on the UNIDROIT Principles of International Commercial Contracts', *Incorporating the UNIDROIT Principles 2004*. 2nd edn. Ardsley, New York: Transnational Publishers, 2006.

Bonell, M.J. 'The UNIDROIT Principles and CISG: Sources of Inspiration for English Courts?' *Uniform Law Review* 11 (2006): 305–318.

Bonell, M.J. *Un codice internazionale del diritto dei contratti: I Principi UNIDROIT dei Contratti Commerciali Internazionali. Aggiornata ai Principi UNIDROIT 2004*. 2nd edn. Milano: Giuffrè, 2006.

Bonell, M.J. 'UNIDROIT Principles 2004: The New Edition of the Principles of International Commercial Contracts Adopted by the International Institute for the Unification of Private Law'. *Beyond Borders: Perspectives on International and Comparative Law*; symposium in honour of Hein Kötz / Faust / Thüsing (eds), Köln; Berlin; Bonn; München: Heymann, 2006.

Bonell, M.J. 'The UNIDROIT Principles a Decade After Their First Appearance: What Have They Achieved and What Are Their Prospects For the Future?' *The UNIDROIT Principles 2004* (2007): 259–265.

Bonell, M.J. & Peleggi, R. 'UNIDROIT Principles of International Commercial Contracts and Draft Common Frame of Reference: A Synoptical Table'. *Uniform Law Review* (2009): 437–554.

Bonell, M.J. 'The New Version of the UNILEX Data Base on the UNIDROIT Principles and the CISG – Upgraded in Form and Enriched in Content'. *National, International, Transnational: Harmonischer Dreiklang im Recht*, 2020, pp. 725–731.

Bortolotti, F. 'The UNIDROIT Principles as a Basis for Alternative Choice-of-Law Clauses, with Particular Reference to the ICC Model Contracts'. *Uniform Law Review*, 19 (2014), pp. 542–549.

Bortolotti, F. 'Towards a Transnational Commercial Law: The Essential Role of the UNIDROIT Principles', edited by UNIDROIT, *Eppur si muove: The Age of Uniform Law. Essays in Honour of Michael Joachim Bonell to Celebrate His 70th Birthday*, Vol. 2 (2016), pp. 1258–1265.

Bouza Vidal, N. 'The UNIDROIT Principles as Legal Background in Spanish Case Law', edited by UNIDROIT, *Eppur si muove: The Age of Uniform Law. Essays in Honour of Michael Joachim Bonell to Celebrate His 70th Birthday*, Vol. 2 (2016), pp. 1266–1282.

Bridge, M.G. 'The CISG and the UNIDROIT Principles of International Commercial Contracts'. *Uniform Law Review*, 19 (2014), pp. 623–642.

Brödermann, E. 'The Growing Importance of the UNIDROIT Principles in Europe: A Review in Light of Market Needs, The Role of Law and The 2005 Rome I Proposal'. *Uniform Law Review* 11 (2006): 749–770.

Brödermann, E. 'The Impact of the UNIDROIT Principles on International Contract and Arbitration Practice: The Experience of a German Lawyer'. *Uniform Law Review* 16 (2011): 3, 589–612.

Brödermann, E. 'The UNIDROIT Principles as a Risk Management Tool', edited by UNIDROIT, *Eppur si muove: The Age of Uniform Law. Essays in Honour of Michael Joachim Bonell to Celebrate His 70th Birthday*, Vol. 2 (2016), pp. 1283–1301.

Brödermann, E. 'Bridge over Troubled Waters for International Commercial Contracts – The UNIDROIT Principles 2016: an overview from a long time user'. *Tulane Journal of International and Comparative Law* [Online], 28 (2020) 2, pp. 193–257.

Selected Bibliography

Brödermann, E. 'UNIDROIT Principles: Warum sie die Vertragsgestaltung bereichern – zehn Thesen: Risikomanagement durch die Wahl der UNIDROIT Principles of International Commercial Contracts 2016' [lange version]. *AnwBl Online*, 2020, pp. 456–469.

Burkart, F. *Interpretatives Zusammenwirken von CISG und UNIDROIT Principles.* Baden-Baden: Nomos Verlagsgesellschaft, 2000 (*Grundlagen und Schwerpunkte des Privatrechts im europäischer Perspektive*, 2).

Carbone, S.M. 'I Principi UNIDROIT quale diritto applicabile ai contratti commerciali internazionali tra autonomia privata e ordinamenti statali'. *Diritto del commercio internazionale* 26 (2012): 47–58.

Caroccia, F. 'L'interpretazione del contratto: il modello dei principi UNIDROIT per i contratti commerciali internazionali nel confronto con le esperienze nazionali'. Napoli: Edizioni Scienifiche Italiane, 2006 (*Quaderni della rassegna di diritto civile*).

Carrara, C. 'The Multiple Usages of the UNIDROIT Principles and the Rules Governing Limitation'. *The Multiple Uses the UNIDROIT Principles of International Commercial Contracts*, 2020, pp. 17–55.

Cemil Yildirim, A. *Equilibrio contrattuale nei Principi UNIDROIT e nel diritto turco.* Roma: Tesi di Laurea, 2007–2008, 222.

Cerini, D. 'Duties and Remedies in the Principles of International Contracts (PICC) and the Principles of Reinsurance Contract Law (PRICL): Notes for a Comparison'. *Uniform Law Review*, 25 (2020) 1, pp. 21–44.

Ciger, S. 'Use of UPICC in Turkish Law: Replies to the Questionnaire on the Use of the UPICC in Order to Interpret or Supplement National Contract Law'. *Use of the UNIDROIT Principles to Interpret and Supplement Domestic Contract Law*, 2021, pp. 335–352.

Corapi, D. 'L'equilibrio delle posizioni contrattuali nei Principi UNIDROIT'. *Europa e Diritto Privato* (2002): 29–40.

Cordero Moss, G. & Behn, D. 'The Relevance of the UNIDROIT Principles in Investment Arbitration'. *Uniform Law Review*, 19 (2014), pp. 570–608.

Cordero-Moss, G. 'Detailed Contract Regulations and the UPICC: Parallels with National Law and Potential for Improvements – The Example of Norwegian Law', in: *Eppur si muove: The Age of Uniform Law. Essays in Honour of Michael Joachim Bonell to Celebrate His 70th Birthday*, edited by UNIDROIT, Vol. 2 (2016), pp. 1302–1317.

Cordero Moss, G. 'The UNIDROIT Principles: long-term contracts'. *The multiple uses of the UNIDROIT Principles of international commercial contracts*, 2020, pp. 75–96.

Crawford, J. & A. Sinclair. 'Application aux contrats de l'État des Principes d'UNIDROIT relatifs aux contrats du commerce international'. *Principes d'UNIDROIT relatifs aux contrats du commerce international. Réflexions sur leur utilisation dans l'arbitrage international, Bulletin de la Cour internationale d'arbitrage de la CCI.* Supplément spécial (2002): 59–79.

Crawford, J. & A. Sinclair. 'The UNIDROIT Principles and Their Application to State contracts'. *UNIDROIT Principles of International Contracts. Reflections on Their Use in International Arbitration, ICC International Court of Arbitration Bulletin.* Special supplement (2002): 57–75.

Crépeau, P.A. 'The UNIDROIT Principles of International Commercial Contracts'. *The Principles of UNIDROIT and Modern National Codifications*, edited by A.M. Rabello. Jerusalem: Harry and Michael Sacher Institute for Legislative Research and Comparative Law, Faculty of Law, The Hebrew University of Jerusalem, 2001.

Dacoronia, E. 'Questionnaire on the Use of the UPICC in Order to Interpret or Supplement National Contract Law: Greece'. *Use of the UNIDROIT Principles to interpret and supplement domestic contract law*, 2021, pp. 173–181.

Darwwas, A. & Kameel, T. 'Applicability of the UNIDROIT Principles as the law governing the merits of arbitration in the gulf cooperation council countries'. 2021 *Arab law quarterly* [Online] London, 1.1985, 35 (2021): 466–487.

Denis, Ph. 'Arbitration, UNIDROIT Principles and the CISG'. *(Best) Practices in arbitration*, 11 (2021), pp. 17–35.

Derains, Y. 'The Role of the UNIDROIT Principles in International Commercial Arbitration (1): A European Perspective'. *UNIDROIT Principles of International Contracts. Reflections on Their Use in International Arbitration, ICC International Court of Arbitration Bulletin*. Special supplement (2002): 9–19.

Dessemontet, F. 'Use of the UNIDROIT Principles to Interpret and Supplement Domestic Law'. *UNIDROIT Principles of International Contracts. Reflections on Their Use in International Arbitration, ICC International Court of Arbitration Bulletin*. Special supplement (2002): 39–50.

Dessemontet, F. 'L'utilisation des Principes UNIDROIT dans le cadre de la pratique contractuelle et de l'activité arbitrale: l'exemple de la Suisse'. *The UNIDROIT Principles 2004* (2007): 159–168.

Deumier, P. 'Les Principes UNIDROIT comme cadre de référence pour l'interprétation uniforme des droits nationaux'. *Études de droit contemporain – Contributions françaises au 20e Congrès international de droit comparé* (Fukuoka, 22–28 juillet 2018). -71 (2019) 2, pp. 413–430.

Deumier, P. 'Les Principes UNIDROIT comme cadre de référence pour l'interprétation uniforme des droits nationaux'. *Use of the UNIDROIT Principles to interpret and supplement domestic contract law*, 2021, pp. 125–149.

Dewey, J. [et al.] 'The Duty to Renegotiate an International Sales Contract under CISG in Case of Hardship and the Use of the UNIDROIT Principles'. *European Review of Private Law* 19 (2011): 1, 101–154.

Doudko, A.G. 'Hardship in Contract: The Approach of the UNIDROIT Principles and Legal Developments in Russia'. *Uniform Law Review* (2000): 483–509.

Drobnig, U. 'Der Stand der internationalen Überlegungen: Die UNIDROIT Principles of International Commercial Contracts'. *Europäisches Kaufgewährleistungsrecht. Reform and Inter-nationalisierung des deutschen Schuldrechts*, edited by S. Grundmann, D. Medicus & Rolland (Hrsg.). Küln, Berlin, Bonn: Carl Heymanns Verlag, 2000.

Eberhard, S. *Les sanctions de l'inexécution du contrat et les Principes UNIDROIT*. Centre du Droit de l'Entreprise (Droit Industriel, Droit d'Auteur, Droit Commercial) de l'Univ. de Lausanne (2005), 527 (Publication CEDIDAC; 63).

Eiselen, S. 'Questionnaire on the Use of the UPICC in Order to Interpret or Supplement National Contract Law: South Africa'. *Use of the UNIDROIT Principles to interpret and supplement domestic contract law*, 2021, pp. 327–333.

Selected Bibliography

Erler, K. & Schmidt-Kessel, M. 'The Use of the UPICC in Order to Interpret or Supplement German Contract Law'. *Use of the UNIDROIT Principles to interpret and supplement domestic contract law*, 2021, pp. 151–172.

Estrella Faria, J.Â. 'The Influence of the UNIDROIT Principles of International Commercial Contracts on National Laws', in: *Eppur si muove: The Age of Uniform Law. Essays in Honour of Michael Joachim Bonell to Celebrate His 70th Birthday*, edited by UNIDROIT, Vol. 2 (2016), pp. 1318–1349.

Farnsworth, A. 'The Role of the UNIDROIT Principles in International Commercial Arbitration (2): A US Perspective on Their Aims and Application'. *UNIDROIT Principles of International Contracts. Reflections on Their Use in International Arbitration, ICC International Court of Arbitration Bulletin*. Special supplement (2002): 21–27.

Fauvarque-Cosson, B. 'The UNIDROIT Principles, the world and the French reform of Contract law', *Eppur si muove: The Age of Uniform Law. Essays in Honour of Michael Joachim Bonell to Celebrate His 70th Birthday*, edited by UNIDROIT, Vol. 2 (2016), pp. 1350–1364.

Fauvarque-Cosson, B. 'Les trois paradoxes des Principes d'UNIDROIT relatifs aux contrats du commerce international. *National, International, Transnational: Harmonischer Dreiklang im Recht*, 2020, pp. 795–802.

Favale, R. 'Conclusion of a contract by offer and acceptance: UNIDROIT Principles and Italian law', UNIDROIT (ed.), *Eppur si muove: The Age of Uniform Law. Essays in Honour of Michael Joachim Bonell to Celebrate His 70th Birthday*, Vol. 2 (2016), pp. 1365–1383.

Ferrari Bravo, L. 'UNIDROIT, l'Organizzazione ed il suo agire: il progetto dei 'Principi dei Contratti Commerciali Internazionali'. *Istituto Giuridico Sammarinese, Miscellanea*, 6 ['I problemi dei contratti' Atti del Seminario organizzato dall'Istituto Giuridico Sammarinese e tenuto in San Marino nell'antico Monastero di Santa Chiara l'8 e il 9 settembre 1998], (2000), 15–28.

Fetze Kamden, I. 'Harmonisation, unification et uniformisation en droit des contrats: plaidoyer pour un discours affiné sur les moyens d'intégration juridique'. *Uniform Law Review*, 13 (2008): 709–744.

Figueroa Valdés, J.E. 'The use of the UNIDROIT Principles by arbitrators in international construction projects'. *Construction law international*, 10 (2015) 1, pp. 24–30.

Finn, P. 'The UNIDROIT Principles: Australia's response'. UNIDROIT (ed.), *Eppur si muove: The Age of Uniform Law. Essays in Honour of Michael Joachim Bonell to Celebrate His 70th Birthday*, Vol. 2 (2016), pp. 1384–1392.

Fontaine, M. 'The UNIDROIT Principles: An Expression of Current Contract Practice?' *UNIDROIT Principles of International Contracts. Reflections on Their Use in International Arbitration, ICC International Court of Arbitration Bulletin*. Special supplement (2002): 95–98.

Fontaine, M. 'Les Principes UNIDROIT et la protection de la partie faible'. *The Future of European Contract Law: Essays In Honour of Ewoud Hondius to Commemorate His Retirement As Professor of Civil Law at the University of Utrecht*, edited by K. Boele-Woelki & W. Grosheide. Alphen aan den Rijn: Kluwer Law International, 2007, 183–193.

Fresnedo de Aguirre, C. 'The UNIDROIT Principles of international commercial contracts: a Uruguayan approach' UNIDROIT (ed.), *Eppur si muove: The Age of Uniform Law. Essays in Honour of Michael Joachim Bonell to Celebrate His 70th Birthday*, Vol. 2 (2016), pp. 1393–1411.

Frick, J.G. 'Die UNIDROIT-Prinzipien für internationale Handelsverträge'. *Recht der Internationalen Wirtschaft*, 47 (2001): 416–422.

Furlanetto, L. & Pagnacco, G. 'The UNIDROIT Principles in EPC contracts of industrial process plants: contractors' experience'. *The multiple uses the UNIDROIT Principles of international commercial contracts*, 2020, pp. 151–180.

Gabriel, H.D. 'An American Perspective on the 2010 UNIDROIT Principles of International Commercial Contracts'. *Rabels Zeitschrift für ausländisches und internationales Privatrecht* 77 (2013): 1, 158–173.

Galizzi, P. 'The versatility of the UNIDROIT Principles for multinational companies: from settling disputes efficiently to enhancing corporate social responsibility'. *The multiple uses the UNIDROIT Principles of international commercial contracts*, 2020, pp. 57–67.

Galizzi, P. & Rojas Egueta, G. & Veneziano, A. [eds.]. - *The multiple uses the UNIDROIT Principles of international commercial contracts: theory and practice*, Milano: Giuffrè (Contratti & commercio internazionale) Francis Lefebvre, 2020, pp. X-261.

Gama, L. da. 'Contratos internacionais à luz dos Princípios do UNIDROIT 2004: soft law, arbitragem e jurisdição'. *Renovar*: Rio de Janeiro (et al.), 2006, 594.

Gama, L. da. 'Os princípios do UNIDROIT na prática arbitral: uma análise de casos (1994–2007)'. *DeCITA, 2008*, 9 (2008): 119–139.

Gama, L. da 'Les usages du commerce dans les Principes d'UNIDROIT'. UNIDROIT (ed.), *Eppur si muove: The Age of Uniform Law. Essays in Honour of Michael Joachim Bonell to Celebrate His 70th Birthday*, Vol. 2 (2016), pp. 1412–1461.

Gama, L. da 'General Considerations on the Interaction of the UPICC and the Brazilian Law'. *Use of the UNIDROIT Principles to interpret and supplement domestic contract law*, 2021, pp. 69–86.

Gama, L. da 'Les Principes d'UNIDROIT et la loi régissant les contrats de commerce international'. *Recueil des cours*, 406 (2020).

Garro, A.M. & Moreno Rodríguez, J.A. [eds.] *Use of the UNIDROIT Principles to interpret and supplement domestic contract law*, Dordrecht: Springer, 2021, pp. ix–409. – (Ius comparatum – global studies in comparative law; 51).

Garro, A.M. & Moreno Rodríguez, J.A. 'The UNIDROIT Principles as a Common Frame of Reference for the Uniform Interpretation of National Laws'. *Use of the UNIDROIT Principles to interpret and supplement domestic contract law*, 2021, pp. 1–38.

Girard, B. *Incidence des règles d'UNIDROIT sur le droit des contrats en Europe*; préface de Muriel Fabre-Magnan. Paris : LGDJ, 2015, pp. XII-405. – (*Bibliothèque de droit privé*; 562).

Glenn, H.P. 'An International Private Law of Contract'. *International Conflict of Laws for the Third Millennium. Essays in Honor of Friedrich K. Juenger*, edited by P.J. Borchers & J. Zekoll. Ardsley, New York: Transnational Publishers, Inc., 2001.

Gordley, J. 'The parol evidence rule and transnational law: the CISG and the UNIDROIT Principles'. UNIDROIT (ed.), *Eppur si muove: The Age of Uniform Law. Essays in Honour of Michael Joachim Bonell to Celebrate His 70th Birthday*, Vol. 2 (2016), pp. 1462–1472.

Gotanda, J.Y. 'Using the UNIDROIT Principles to Fill Gaps in the CISG'. *Contract Damages: Domestic and International Perspectives*, ed. D Saidov & R Cunnington. (2008), 107–122.

Grigera Naón, H. 'Closing Remarks'. *UNIDROIT Principles of International Contracts. Reflections on Their Use in International Arbitration, ICC International Court of Arbitration Bulletin.* Special supplement (2002): 149–151.

Grigera Naón, H.A. 'UNIDROIT Principles as Proper Law. *National, International, Transnational: Harmonischer Dreiklang im Recht*, 2020, pp. 121–127.

Gwynn, M.A. 'Contratos internacionales para el sector privado: estudio comparativo entre Principios de UNIDROIT y el Mercosur'. Asunción: *El Lector*, 2007, 173. (*Colección sociedad y economia*).

Han, S. 'The UNIDROIT Principles and the development of the Chinese contract law'. UNIDROIT (ed.), *Eppur si muove: The Age of Uniform Law. Essays in Honour of Michael Joachim Bonell to Celebrate His 70th Birthday*, Vol. 2 (2016), pp. 1473–1485.

Heggberget, L.M. & E. Nyland. 'Formuleringen av internasjonale kontraktsrettslige grunnprinsipper og betydningen for norsk rett'. *Tidsskrift for Rettsvitenskap* (2000): 251–323.

Hepburn, J. 'The UNIDROIT Principles of international commercial contracts and investment treaty arbitration: a limited relationship'. *The International and Comparative Law Quarterly*, 64 (2015) 4, pp. 905–933.

Hernández-Bretón, E. & Madrid Martínez, C. 'Use of the UPICC in Order to Interpret or Supplement National Contract Law: Venezuela. *Use of the UNIDROIT Principles to interpret and supplement domestic contract law*, 2021, pp. 395–409.

Hinestrosa, F. 'De los principios generales del derecho a los principios generales del contrato'. *Revista de Derecho Privado* (2000): 5, 3–22.

Houtte, H. van 'Compensation for future harm – Article 7.4.3 UNIDROIT Principles'. UNIDROIT (ed.), *Eppur si muove: The Age of Uniform Law. Essays in Honour of Michael Joachim Bonell to Celebrate His 70th Birthday*, Vol. 2 (2016), pp. 1486–1492.

Houtte, H. van 'Contract negotiations and the UNIDROIT Principles'. *Uniform Law Review*, 19 (2014), pp. 550–560.

ICC (ed.). 'Principes d'UNIDROIT relatifs aux contrats du commerce international. Réflexions sur leur utilisation dans l'arbitrage international'. *Bulletin de la Cour Internationale d'arbitrage de la CCI.* Supplément spécial, Paris: ICC Publishing S.A., 2002, 167 (N° CCI: publication 642F).

ICC (ed.). *UNIDROIT Principles of International Contracts. Reflections on Their Use in International Arbitration, ICC International Court of Arbitration Bulletin.* Special supplement, Paris: ICC Publishing S.A., 2002, 155 (ICC Publication No. 642E).

Institut Suisse de Droit Comparé <Lausanne>. 'The UNIDROIT Principles 2004: Their impact on contractual practice, jurisprudence and codification. *Reports of the ISDC Colloquium (8/9 June 2006)*, Swiss Institute of Comparative Law, Zürich: Schulthess, 2004. 265 (*Publications de l'Institut Suisse de Droit Comparé*; 56).

Institute of International Banking Law and Practice (ed.). *Restatement 2d Contracts & UNIDROIT Principles: The Texts, The Comments & The Illustrations*. Student Texts including Comments and Illustrations. Montgomery Village. Maryland: Institute of International Banking Law and Practice, Inc. Publications, 2001.

Institutul InternaȚional pentru Unificarea Dreptului Privat. *Principiile UNIDROIT: Aplicabile Contractelor Comerciale InternaȚionale*. Traducere De Marilena Ene Şi Laura Oprea; PrefaȚa De Eugen Vasiliu., 2004., Bucureşti 2006: Editura Minerva, 2006.

Instituto Internacional para la Unificación del Derecho Privado. *Principios UNIDROIT Sobre Los Contratos Comerciales Internacionales 2004*. 2nd edn. México: Inst. de Investigaciones Jur., Centro Mexicano de Derecho Uniforme, 2007.

Ius, M. 'Possible applications of the UNIDROIT Principles in international construction contracts: what about the updated 2017 FIDIC yellow book? *The multiple uses the UNIDROIT Principles of International Commercial Contracts*, 2020, pp. 181–199.

Jacquet, J.-M. 'Le droit français des contrats et les Principes UNIDROIT'. *L'harmonisation du droit OHADA des contrats* (2008): 179–195.

Jolivet, E. 'L'harmonisation du droit OHADA des contrats: l'influence des principes d'UNIDROIT en matière de pratique contractuelle et d'arbitrage'. *L'harmonisation du droit OHADA des contrats* (2008): 127–152.

Jung, P. 'Der Einfluss der UNIDROIT Principles auf das Gemeinschaftsprivatrecht'. *The UNIDROIT Principles 2004* (2007): 77–91.

Király, M. 'The UNIDROIT Principles as Reference for the Uniform Interpretation of National Laws: Report on Hungarian Law. *Use of the UNIDROIT Principles to interpret and supplement domestic contract law*, 2021, pp. 195–208.

Komarov, A.S. 'Reference to the UNIDROIT Principles in international commercial arbitration practice in the Russian Federation'. *Uniform Law Review* 16 (2011): 3, 657–667.

Komarov, A.S. 'The UNIDROIT Principles of international commercial contracts and the development of contract law in modern Russia'. UNIDROIT (ed.), *Eppur si muove: The Age of Uniform Law. Essays in Honour of Michael Joachim Bonell to Celebrate His 70th Birthday*, Vol. 2 (2016), pp. 1493–1502.

Kotrusz, J. 'Gap-filling of the CISG by the UNIDROIT Principles of International Commercial Contracts'. *Uniform Law Review* (2009): 119–163.

Kramer, E.A. & T. Probst. 'Defects in the Contracting Process'. Chapter II of Vol. II, *Contracts in General* (ed. A. von Mehren). Tübingen: Mohr Siebeck, 2001. *International Encyclopedia of Comparative Law.*

Kronke, H, 'Introduction'. *UNIDROIT Principles of International Contracts. Reflections on Their Use in International Arbitration, ICC International Court of Arbitration Bulletin*. Special supplement (2002): 7–8.

Kronke, H. 'The UN Sales Convention, the UNIDROIT Contract Principles and the Way Beyond'. *The Journal of Law and Commerce* 25 (2005): 1, 451–465.

Selected Bibliography

Kronke, H. 'Opening of the Colloquium'. *The UNIDROIT Principles 2004* (2007): 13–15.

Lalive, P. 'The UNIDROIT Principles As *Lex Contractus*, with or without an Explicit or Tacit Choice of Law: An Arbitror's Perspective'. *UNIDROIT Principles of International Contracts. Reflections on Their Use in International Arbitration, ICC International Court of Arbitration Bulletin*. Special supplement (2002): 77–83.

Lando, O. 'A Vision of a Future World of Contract Law-impact of European and UNIDROIT Contract Principles'. *Uniform Commercial Code Law Journal* 37 (2004): 2, 1–38.

Lando, O. 'Termination for Breach Contract in the CISG, the Principles of European Contract Law, the UNIDROIT Principles of International Commercial Contracts'. *The Future of European Contract Law: Essays in Honour of Ewoud Hondius to Commemorate His Retirement as Professor of Civil Law at the University of Utrecht*, edited by K. Boele-Woelki & W. Grosheide. Alphen aan den Rijn: Kluwer Law International, 2007.

Leduc, A. 'L'émergence d'une nouvelle *lex mercatoria* à l'enseigne des Principes d'UNIDROIT relatifs aux contrats du commerce international: thèse et antithèse'. *Revue Juridique Thémis* 35 (2001): 429–451.

Lein, E. 'La portée pratique des Principes UNIDROIT: une perspective allemande'. *The UNIDROIT Principles 2004* (2007): 169–188.

Lein, E. 'L'effet harmonisateur des Principes UNIDROIT et ses limites'. *L'harmonisation internationale du droit*, ed. C. Chappuis (2007), 171–189.

Lerner, P. 'The Principles of International Commercial Contracts as model law: an Israeli perspective'. *Uniform Law Review*, 24 (2019) 1, pp. 121–148.

Les Principes d'UNIDROIT relatifs aux contrats du commerce international: réflexions sur leur utilisation dans l'arbitrage international, Supplément spécial 2002. *Bulletin de la Cour Internationale d'Arbitrage de la CCI* : 165.

Letterman, G.G. *UNIDROIT's Rules in Practice. Standard International Contracts and Applicable Rules*. The Hague: Kluwer Law International, 2001.

Lew, J.D.M. 'The UNIDROIT Principles as *Lex Contractus* Chosen by the Parties and Without an Explicit Choice-of-Law Clause: The Perspective of Counsel'. *UNIDROIT Principles of International Contracts. Reflections on Their Use in International Arbitration, ICC International Court of Arbitration Bulletin*. Special supplement (2002): 9–19.

Lopez de Gonzalo, M. 'I punitive damages nel diritto internazionale privato, nel diritto uniforme e nei Principi UNIDROIT'. UNIDROIT (ed.), *Eppur si muove: The Age of Uniform Law. Essays in Honour of Michael Joachim Bonell to Celebrate His 70th Birthday*, Vol. 2 (2016), pp. 1503–1519.

Magnus, U. 'Die UNIDROIT Principles und die Wiener Kaufrechtskonvention'. *The UNIDROIT Principles 2004* (2007): 57–64.

Maile-Zinser, T. *Auswirkungen der Unmöglichkeit auf den Erfüllungsanspruch: eine rechtsvergleichende Untersuchung zum deutschen Recht, dem US-amerikanischen Uniform Commercial Code, dem UN-Kaufrecht, den UNIDROIT Principles of International Commercial Contracts, den Principles of European Contract Law und dem Vorentwurf eines europäischen Vertragsgesetzbuch*. Berlin: Logos, 2006.

Malaguti, M.C. & Finazzi Agrò, E. 'L'utilizzo dei principi UNIDROIT nell'arbitrato internazionale di investimento, *Arbitrato, contratti e diritto del commercio internazionale*. 2021. Milano: 489–509.

Mankowski, P. [ed.] *Commercial law: article-by-article commentary* Baden-Baden: Nomos; München, 2019. pp. XLV, 1531. (Nomos). (International and European Business Law).

Marcenaro, E. 'An in-house counsel activity in the power generation sector: dispute management under EPC contracts'. *The multiple uses the UNIDROIT Principles of international commercial contracts*, 2020, pp. 127–149.

Marella, F. 'Nuovi sviluppi dei Principi UNIDROIT sui Contratti Commerciali Internazionali nell'arbitrato CCI'. *Contratto e Impresa/Europa* 7 (2002): 40–53.

Mariño López, A. 'Questionnaire on the Use of the UPICC in Order to Interpret or Supplement National Contract Law: Uruguay'. *Use of the UNIDROIT Principles to interpret and supplement domestic contract law*, 2021, pp. 353–360.

Marrella, F. '*Lex mercatoria* e Principi UNIDROIT. Per una ricostruzione sistematica del diritto del commercio internazionale'. *Contratto e Impresa/Europa* 5 (2000): 29–79.

Marrella, F. 'The UNIDROIT Principles of International Commercial Contracts in ICC arbitration 1999–2001'. *ICC International Court of Arbitration Bulletin* 12 (2001): 49–55; Extracts from ICC awards referring to the UNIDROIT Principles of International Commercial Contracts, 56–115.

Marrella, F. 'Contratti di vendita internazionale privi di prezzo, questione preliminare e Principi UNIDROIT'. *Rivista dell'Arbitrato* 12 (2002): 130–138.

Martínez Cañellas, A. 'The Influence of the UNIDROIT Principles on the Proposal of the Reform of the Spanish Commercial Code'. *The UNIDROIT Principles 2004* (2007): 215–229.

Mayer, P. 'The Role of the UNIDROIT Principles in ICC Arbitration Practice'. *UNIDROIT Principles of International Contracts. Reflections on Their Use in International Arbitration, ICC International Court of Arbitration Bulletin*. Special supplement (2002): 105–117.

Mendoza Montano, P. & Martínez Guzmán, E. 'The UNIDROIT Principles of International Commercial Contracts (UPICC) as Reference for the Uniform Interpretation of Guatemalan Law'. *Use of the UNIDROIT Principles to interpret and supplement domestic contract law*, 2021, pp. 183–193.

Michaels, R. 'Umdenken für die UNIDROIT-Prinzipien: Vom Rechtswahlstatut zum Allgemeinen Teil des transnationalen Vertragsrechts'. *Rabels Zeitschrift für ausländisches und internationales Privatrecht* 73 (2009): 866–888.

Michaels, R. 'The UNIDROIT Principles as Reference for the Interpretation of US Law'. *Use of the UNIDROIT Principles to interpret and supplement domestic contract law*, 2021, pp. 361–394.

Mo, J.S. 'The UNIDROIT Principles of international commercial contracts in Chinese judicial practice'. UNIDROIT (ed.), *Eppur si muove: The Age of Uniform Law. Essays in Honour of Michael Joachim Bonell to Celebrate His 70th Birthday*, Vol. 2 (2016), pp. 1542–1553.

Momberg Uribe, R. 'The UNIDROIT Principles as Reference for the Uniform Interpretation of National Laws: Chile'. *Use of the UNIDROIT Principles to interpret and supplement domestic contract law*, 2021, pp. 87–91.

Selected Bibliography

Moreno Rodríguez, J.A. 'The UNIDROIT Principles of International Commercial Contracts (UPICC) as Reference for the Uniform Interpretation of Paraguayan Law'. *Use of the UNIDROIT Principles to interpret and supplement domestic contract law*, 2021, pp. 273–301.

Muñoz, A. & Geny, D. 'Les Principes d'UNIDROIT dans l'arbitrage international = The UNIDROIT Principles in international arbitration'. *Revue de droit des affaires internationales = International business law journal*, 2 (2016), pp. 109–117.

Nguyen, T.V.H. 'Le rôle des Principes d'UNIDROIT relatifs aux contrats de commerce international et une expérience pour le Vietnam' (Mémoire présenté et soutenu pour l'obtention du Master 2 'Droit international et Droit comparé' par Thi Viet Ha Nguyen) Toulouse, 2005–2006, 82 (Thèse, Toulouse).

Onana Etoundi, F. 'Les Principes d' UNIDROIT et la sécurité juridique des transactions commerciales dans l'avant-projet d'Acte uniforme OHADA sur les contrats'. *Uniform Law Review* 10 (2005): 683–718.

Oser, D. *The UNIDROIT Principles of International Commercial Contracts: A Governing Law*. Leiden: Martinus Nijhoff Publishers, 2008.

Oviedo Albán, J. 'La cesión de la posición contractual en el derecho colombiano y los Principios de UNIDROIT'. *DeCITA* 9 (2008): 140–149.

Pauknerová, M. 'The UNIDROIT Principles and Czech law'. UNIDROIT (ed.), *Eppur si muove: The Age of Uniform Law. Essays in Honour of Michael Joachim Bonell to Celebrate His 70th Birthday*, Vol. 2 (2016), pp. 1583–1592.

Pauknerová, M. & Pfeiffer, M. 'UNIDROIT Principles as Reference for Uniform Interpretation of National Laws: Czech Republic'. *Use of the UNIDROIT Principles to interpret and supplement domestic contract law*, 2021, pp. 101–123.

Peleggi, R. 'Sui principi latinoamericani del diritto dei contratti'. *Principi e regole per una società globale*, 2019, pp. 281–301.

Perales Viscasillas, P. 'Los Principios de UNIDROIT en la jurisprudencia del Tribunal Supremo español'. UNIDROIT (ed.), *Eppur si muove: The Age of Uniform Law. Essays in Honour of Michael Joachim Bonell to Celebrate His 70th Birthday*, Vol. 2 (2016), pp. 1619–1639.

Petz, T. *Die UNIDROIT Prinzipien für internationale Handelsverträge*. Verlag Österreich, 2001, 261 (*Juristische Schriftenreihe*, Band 177).

Portmann, U. 'Alles was Recht ist – Die Rechtswahl der UNIDROIT-Prinzipien und deren Lückenfüllung im schweizerischen IPRG'. *The UNIDROIT Principles 2004* (2007): 191–200.

Principes d'UNIDROIT: nouvelles évolutions et applications, Supplément spécial 2005. *Bulletin de la Cour Internationale d'Arbitrage de la CCI :* 97.

Probst, T. 'The UNIDROIT Principles of International Commercial Contracts 1994 and 2004: A Brief Introduction with a Synoptic Overview'. *The UNIDROIT Principles 2004* (2007): 17–22.

Rabello, A.M. (ed.). *The Principles of UNIDROIT and Modern National Codifications*. Jerusalem: Harry and Michael Sacher Institute for Legislative Research and Comparative Law, Faculty of Law, The Hebrew University of Jerusalem, 2001.

Rabello, A.M. & P. Lerner. 'The UNIDROIT Principles of International Contracts and Israeli law [in Hebrew]'. *The Principles of UNIDROIT and Modern National Codifications*, edited by A.M. Rabello. Jerusalem: Harry and Michael Sacher Institute for Legislative Research and Comparative Law, Faculty of Law, The Hebrew University of Jerusalem, 2001.

Raeschke-Kessler, H. 'The UNIDROIT Principles in Contemporary Contract Practice'. *UNIDROIT Principles of International Contracts. Reflections on Their Use in International Arbitration, ICC International Court of Arbitration Bulletin.* Special supplement (2002): 99–104.

Ramberg, C. 'The rules on standard terms in the UNIDROIT Principles: misplaced and misleading'. UNIDROIT (ed.), *Eppur si muove: The Age of Uniform Law. Essays in honour of Michael Joachim Bonell to Celebrate His 70th Birthday*, Vol. 2 (2016), pp. 1640–1648.

Ramberg, C. 'The UNIDROIT Principles as a means of interpreting domestic law'. *Uniform Law Review*, 19 (2014), pp. 669–675.

Reinisch, A. 'The relevance of the UNIDROIT Principles of International Commercial Contracts in international investment arbitration' *Uniform Law Review*, 19 (2014), pp. 609–622.

Remien, O. 'Die UNIDROIT-Prinzipien und die Grundregeln des Europäischen Vertragsrechts: ein vergleichender Blick'. *The UNIDROIT Principles 2004* (2007): 65–76. M. Oudin.

Rivera, J.C. 'The Use of the UNIDROIT Principles of International Commercial Contracts in Order to Interpret or Supplement Argentine Contract Law'. *Use of the UNIDROIT Principles to interpret and supplement domestic contract law*, 2021, pp. 39–53.

Rojas Egueta, G. 'From "antagonistic" to "empathic": the long-term contracts' continuum and the role of UNIDROIT Principles. *The multiple uses the UNIDROIT Principles of international commercial contracts*, 2020, pp. 97–123.

Rojas Egueta, G. 'Postscript to part I: the use of the UNIDROIT Principles in Italy'. *The multiple uses the UNIDROIT Principles of international commercial contracts*, 2020, pp. 69–71.

Rongeat-Oudin, F. & M. Oudin. 'La réception des Principes UNIDROIT par la *Lex Mercatoria*: l'exemple de la bonne foi = The reception of the UNIDROIT Principles by the lex mercatoria: the example of good faith'. *Revue de droit des affaires internationales*, 2009.

Romano, G.P. 'Le choix des Principes UNIDROIT par les contractants à l'épreuve des dispositions impératives'. *The UNIDROIT Principles 2004* (2007): 35–54.

Rueda, I. *Incidence des règles d'UNIDROIT sur le droit des contrats en Europe*; avant-propos de Herbert Kronke; préface de Sylvaine Poillot Peruzzeto. Paris: L.G.D.J., 2015, pp. XXII-545. (*Bibliothèque de droit privé*; 559).

Saidov, D. 'Causation in Damages: The Convention on Contracts for the International Sale of Goods, the UNIDROIT Principles of International Commercial Contracts, the Principles of European Contract Law'. *Review of the Convention on Contracts for the International Sale of Goods (CISG), 2004* (2005): 225–267.

Saidov, D. 'Anticipatory Non-performance and Underlying Values of the UNIDROIT Principles'. *Uniform Law Review* 11 (2006): 795–823.

Sandrock, O. 'Die objektive Anknüpfung von Verträgen nach § 1051 Abs. 2 ZPO'. *Recht der Internationalen Wirtschaft* 46 (2000): 321–328.

Schinkels, B. 'Die (Un-)Zulässigkeit einer kollisionsrechtlichen Wahl der UNIDROIT Principles nach Rom I'. *GPR* 4 (2007): 1, 106–111.

Schlechtriem, P. 'Abstandnahme Vom Vertrag'. In *Europäische Vertragsrechtsvereinheitlichung und deutsches Recht*, edited by J. Basedow. Tübingen: Mohr Siebeck, 2000.

Schwartze, A. 'The UNIDROIT Principles as Reference for the Uniform Interpretation of National Laws: National Report Austria'. *Use of the UNIDROIT Principles to interpret and supplement domestic contract law*, 2021, pp. 55–67.

Schwenzer, I.H. & Muñoz, E. 'Duty to renegotiate and contract adaptation in case of hardship'. *Uniform Law Review*, 24 (2019) 1, pp. 149–174.

Shirvindt, A.M. 'The UNIDROIT Principles as Reference for the Uniform Interpretation of National Laws: National Report for Russian Federation'. *Use of the UNIDROIT Principles to interpret and supplement domestic contract law*, 2021, pp. 303–325.

Siehr, K. 'Die UNIDROIT Principles of international commercial contracts und Irrtum beim Handel mit Kulturgütern'. UNIDROIT (ed.), *Eppur si muove: The Age of Uniform Law. Essays in Honour of Michael Joachim Bonell to Celebrate His 70th Birthday*, Vol. 2 (2016), pp. 1664–1674.

Simonelli, U. 'The UNIDROIT Principles in the automotive sector'. *The multiple uses the UNIDROIT Principles of international commercial contracts*, 2020, pp. 201–212.

Skala, J. 'The UNIDROIT Principles of International Commercial Contracts: A Russian Perspective'. *The UNIDROIT Principles 2004* (2007): 119–133.

Sono, H. & Morishita, T. 'The UNIDROIT Principles as reference for the uniform interpretation of national laws: the case of Japan'. *Japanese reports for the XXth International Congress of Comparative Law* (Fukuoka, 22–28 July 2018), 2019, pp. 13–35.

Sono, H. & Morishita, T. 'The UNIDROIT Principles as Reference for the Uniform Interpretation of National Laws: The Case of Japan'. *Use of the UNIDROIT Principles to interpret and supplement domestic contract law*, 2021, pp. 243–271.

Sychold, M. 'The Impact of the UNIDROIT Contract Principles on Australian Law'. *The UNIDROIT Principles 2004* (2007): 149–156.

Teichert, U. *Lückenfüllung im CISG mittels UNIDROIT-Prinzipien: zugleich ein Beitrag zur Wählbarkeit nichtstaatlichen Rechts*. Frankfurt am Main; Berlin; Bern; Wien et al.: Peter Lang, 2007. LXXIII-300 (*Studien zum vergleichenden und internationalen Recht*; 129).

Tercier, P. 'Schiedsgerichtsbarkeit und "Principles"'. *Zeitschrift für Europäisches Privatrecht* 18 (2010): 229–242.

Tobar Torres, J.A. 'Los principios UNIDROIT: fundamentos, práctica y aplicaciones'. Ibañez, Bogotá: pp. 352.

Toth, O. 'The UNIDROIT Principles of International Commercial Contracts as the Governing law: Reflections in Light of the Reform of the Rome Convention'. *The UNIDROIT Principles 2004* (2007): 201–213.

Traisci, F.P. 'Hardship e force majeure nei contratti del commercio internazionale: un modello innovativo da seguire'. UNIDROIT (ed.), *Eppur si muove: The Age of*

Uniform Law. Essays in Honour of Michael Joachim Bonell to Celebrate His 70th Birthday, Vol. 2 (2016), pp. 1675–1686.

Veillard, I. 'Le caractère général et commercial des Principes d'UNIDROIT relatifs aux contrats du commerce international'. *The UNIDROIT Principles 2004* (2007): 23–34.

Veillard, I. 'Le caractère général et commercial des Principes d'UNIDROIT relatifs aux contrats du commerce international'. *Revue de droit des affaires internationales* (2007): 479–492.

Veneziano, A. & Finazzi Agrò, E. 'The use of the UNIDROIT Principles in order to interpret or supplement national law: an Italian perspective'. *The multiple uses the UNIDROIT Principles of international commercial contracts*, 2020, pp. 5–16.

Veneziano, A. & Finazzi Agró, E. 'Italian National Report on the Use of the UPICC in Order to Interpret or Supplement National Contract Law'. *Use of the UNIDROIT Principles to interpret and supplement domestic contract law*, 2021, pp. 209–241.

Vitucci, P. 'L'atto unilaterale nei Principles e in altre compilazioni sul diritto europeo dei contratti'. *Studi in onore di Giuseppe Benedetti* (2008): 2179–2187.

Vogenauer, S. & J. Kleinheisterkamp (eds). *Commentary on the UNIDROIT Principles of International Commercial Contracts (PICC).* Oxford: Oxford University Press, 2009.

Vogenauer, S. 'Interpretation of the UNIDROIT Principles of International Commercial Contracts by National Courts'. *Content and Meaning of National Law in Context of Transnational Law*, edited by H. Snijders & S. Vogenauer. Munich: Sellier, 2009.

Vogenauer, S. 'Termination of long-term contracts "for Compelling Reasons" under the UNIDROIT Principles: the German origins'. UNIDROIT (ed.), *Eppur si muove: The Age of Uniform Law. Essays in Honour of Michael Joachim Bonell to Celebrate His 70th Birthday*, Vol. 2 (2016), pp. 1698–1716.

Vogenauer, S. 'The UNIDROIT Principles of International Commercial Contracts at twenty: experiences to date, the 2010 edition, and future prospects' *Uniform Law Review*, 19 (2014), pp. 481–518.

Volders, B. 'The UNIDROIT Principles of International Commercial Contracts and Dutch Law'. *The UNIDROIT Principles 2004* (2007): 135–148.

Weidemann, C. *Lückenergänzung and richterliche Fortbildung nach Art. 1.6. II der UNIDROIT – Principles for International Commercial Contracts. Methode und Beispiele: Rückgewährschuldverhältnisse, postvertragliche Pflichten, objektive Beweislast.* Frankfurt a. M., Berlin: Bern, Peter Lang, 2001 (*Europäische Hochschulschriften. Reihe II. Rechtswissenschaft*, 3213).

Weintraub, R.J. '*Lex mercatoria* and the UNIDROIT Principles of International Commercial Contracts'. *International Conflict of Laws for the Third Millennium. Essays in Honor of Friedrich K. Juenger*, edited by P.J. Borchers, J. Zekoll. Ardsley, New York: Transnational Publishers, Inc. 2001.

Wolf, M. 'Willensmängel und sonstige Beeinträchtigungen der Entscheidungsfreiheit in einem europäischen Vertragsrecht'. *Europäische Vertragsrechtsvereinheitlichung und deutsches Recht*, edited by J. Basedow. Tübingen: Mohr Siebeck, 2000.

Xi, J. 'The Impact of the UNIDROIT Principles on Chinese Legislation'. *The UNIDROIT Principles 2004* (2007): 107–118.

You, Chin-Fa & Hsiao, Chia-Te 'The UNIDROIT Principles as Reference for the Uniform Interpretation of National Laws: China'. *Use of the UNIDROIT Principles to interpret and supplement domestic contract law*, 2021, pp. 93–100.

Zhang, S. 'L'influence des Principes d'UNIDROIT sur la réforme du droit chinois des obligations'. *L'harmonisation du droit OHADA des contrats* (2008): 153–178.

Zhang, Y. & D.Huang. 'The New Contract Law in the People's Republic of China and the UNIDROIT Principles of International Commercial Contracts: A brief comparison'. *Uniform Law Review* (2000): 429–440.

Zimmermann, R. '*Restitutio in Integrum*: The Unwinding of Failed Contracts under the Principles of European Contract Law, the UNIDROIT Principles and the Avant-projet d'un Code européen des contrats'. *Uniform Law Review* 10 (2005): 719–735.

Zimmermann, R. 'The Significance of the Principles of European Contract Law'. *European Review of Private Law*, 28 (2020) 3, pp. 487–496.

Žukas, T. 'Reception of the UNIDROIT Principles of International Commercial Contracts and the Principles of European Contract Law in Lithuania'. *The UNIDROIT Principles 2004* (2007): 231–243.

Agency

Diloy, C. *Le contrat d'agence commerciale en droit international.* Paris: Librairie Générale de Droit et de Jurisprudence, 2000 (*Bibliothèque de droit privé*, Tome 334).

Leasing

Adame Goddard, J. 'Convención de UNIDROIT sobre Arrendamiento Financiero Internacional'. *Revista de Derecho Privado* (Instituto de Investigaciones Jurídicas, Universidad Nacional Autónoma de México), 5 (1994), Núms. 13, 14 y 15, 159.

Bakkour, E.M. 'Une lecture de la Convention d'UNIDROIT sur le crédit-bail international (Ottawa, 28 mai 1988)'. *Revue marocaine de Droit et d'Economie du développement* 1994), N° 34, 103.

Béguin, J. 'Une tentative d'équilibrage contractuel: la Convention d'Ottawa sur le crédit-bail mobilier international'. *Études offertes à Jacques Ghestin. Le contrat au début du XXIe siècle*, 65–90. Paris: Librairie Générale de Droit et de Jurisprudence, 2001.

Bey, El-Mokhtar. 'Les rapports des parties dans la Loi type d'UNIDROIT sur la location et la location-financement'. *Uniform Law Review* (2009): 601–624.

Castillo-Triana, R. 'Equipment Leasing: Trends and Regulations in Latin America – A Case for the UNIDROIT Leasing Convention'. *Uniform Law Review* 7 (2002): 737–750.

Clarizia, R. 'La Convenzione UNIDROIT sulla locazione finanziaria: analogie e differenze rispetto al modello italiano'. *Rivista di Diritto dell'Impresa* (1994): 27.

Cuming, R.C.C. 'Model Rules for Lease Financing: a Possible Complement to the UNIDROIT Convention on International Financial Leasing'. Uniform Law Studies in memory of Malcolm Evans, *Uniform Law Review* 2, no. 3 (1998): 371–384.

Dageforde, C. 'Inkrafttreten der UNIDROIT-Konvention von Ottawa vom 28. 5. 1988 über Internationales Finanzierungsleasing'. *Recht der Internationalen Wirtschaft* 41 (1995): 265.

Dalhuisen, J.H. 'The UNIDROIT Convention on International Financial Leasing'. *Eenvormig en Vergelijkend Privaatrecht* (1994): 27.

De Nova, G. 'La défaillance du crédit-preneur sous l'empire de la Convention d'UNIDROIT sur le crédit-bail international'. *Uniform Law Review* (1996): 255.

Dekoven, R. 'The Conceptual Approach Followed by the UNIDROIT Model Law on Leasing'. *Uniform Law Review* (2009): 625–629.

Fötschl, A. 'Financial Leasing unter der UNIDROIT-Convention on International Financial Leasing und dem Draft Common Frame of Reference: Eine Vergleichende Analyse'. *European Review of Private Law* 17 no. 4 (2009): 659–673.

Girsberger, D. *Grenzüberschreitendes Finanzierungsleasing* (Max-Planck-Institut für aus-ländisches und internationales Privatrecht. Beiträge zum ausländischen und internationale Privatrecht, 61). Tübingen: Mohr Siebeck.

Goode, R.M. 'Practical Questions Relating to the UNIDROIT Convention on International Financial Leasing'. *Uniform Commercial Law in the Twenty-first Century, 106. Proceedings of the Congress of the United Nations Commission on International Trade Law*, New York, 18–22 May 1992. New York, United Nations, 1995.

Hauck, B. 'The Scope of the UNIDROIT Model Law on Leasing'. *Uniform Law Review* (2009): 631–635.

Honnebier, B.P. 'Het Effect Van De UNIDROIT Convention on International Financial Leasing in Nederland'. *Weekblad voor Privaatrecht, Notariaat en Registratie* 127 (1996): 755–776.

Honnebier, B.P. 'Het aansprakelijkheidsregime van de UNIDROIT Convention on International Financial Leasing'. *Tussen de polen van bescherming en vrijheid. Aspecten van aansprakelijkheid*, 92 et seq. Opstellen geschreven ter gelegenheid van het feit dat het Molengraaff Instituut voor Privaatrecht in 1998 gedurende 40 jaar de naam van Molengraaf draagt. Interscientia Rechtswetenschappen.

Knebel, A. 'Der Aufwendungsersatzanspruch des Leasinggebers nach der UNIDROIT-Leasing-Konvention'. Bern: Lang, 1994.

Kronke, H. 'Financial Leasing and Its Unification by UNIDROIT'. *General Reports of the XVIIIth Congress of the International Academy of Comparative Law*, 2012, 321–333.

La Torre, M.R. 'Il Leasing Finanziario Internazionale'. In Manuale della locazione finanziaria, edited by M.R. La Torre. Milano: Giuffrè, 2002.

Levy, D.A. 'Financial Leasing under the UNIDROIT Convention and the Uniform Commercial Code: A Comparative Analysis'. *Indiana International and Comparative Law Review* 5 (1995): 267.

Leyva Saavedra, J. 'La Convención del UNIDROIT sobre el leasing internacional'. Leyva Saavedra, J. *Contratos de empresa, Tomo I*, 375–387 (*Tratado de derecho privado, Volumen II*), Lima: Editorial San Marcos, 1997.

Leyva Saavedra, J. 'La Convención del UNIDROIT sobre el leasing internacional'. Leyva Saavedra, J. *Leasing*, 391–413 (*Tratado de derecho privado, Volumen I*), Lima: Editorial San Marcos, 1998.

Llinas Volpe, M.A. 'Convenio de UNIDROIT sobre arrendamiento financiero internacional adoptado en Ottawa el 26 de mayo de 1988' (Introducción), *Acuerdos internacionales de facilitación del Comercio Internacional*, Ministerio de Justicia y del Derecho de la República de Colombia, 1997, 87–101.

Mariani, P. 'Il leasing finanziario internazionale uniforme e il diritto internazionale privato'. *Rivista di diritto internazionale / Studi e pubblicazioni; 60.* Padova: Cedam, 2004, XIV–198.

Mooney, C.W. 'Exporting UCC Article 9 to an International Convention: The Local Law Conundrum'. *Canadian Business Law Journal* 27 (1996): 278.

Schermi, A. 'Il leasing finanziario e la Convenzione internazionale di Ottawa 28 maggio 1988, resa esecutiva con l. 14 luglio 1993, n. 259', *Giustizia Civile* 44 (1994), I, 725.

Schwarz, S. 'Das Internationale Stellvertretungsrecht im Spiegel nationaler und supranationaler Kodifikationen'. *Rabels Zeitschrift für ausländisches und internationales Privatrecht* 71 (2007): 729–800.

Stanford, M.J. 'Recent Developments with the UNIDROIT Convention'. *World Leasing Yearbook* (1994): 46.

Stanford, M.J. 'Recent Developments with the UNIDROIT Convention'. *World Leasing Yearbook* (1995): 41.

Stanford, M.J. 'UNIDROIT Convention on Leasing Enters into Force'. *World Leasing Yearbook* (1996): 28.

Stanford, M.J. 'International Financial Leasing: The Status of the UNIDROIT Convention and an Analysis of its Provisions'. *Uniform Commercial Code Law Journal* 32 (Fall 1999): 182–205.

Stanford, M.J. 'The UNIDROIT Convention on International Financial Leasing'. *World Leasing Yearbook* (1999): 32–35.

Stanford, M.J. 'The UNIDROIT Convention on International Financial Leasing'. *World Leasing Yearbook* (2000): 40–43.

Stanford, M.J. 'The UNIDROIT Convention on International Financial Leasing'. *World Leasing Yearbook* (2001): 40–43.

Stanford, M.J. 'From Ottawa to Cape Town: UNIDROIT's Role in the Modernisation of the Law Governing Leasing and the Taking of Security'. *Security Interests in Mobile Equipment*, ed. I. Davies. Aldershot: Dartmouth Publishing Company, Ashgate Publishing Limited, 2002, 397–448.

Stanford, M.J. 'UNIDROIT's Preparation of a Model Law on Leasing: the Crossing of New Frontiers in the Making of Uniform Law'. *Uniform Law Review* (2009): 578–599.

Sultanov, M. 'The UNIDROIT Model Law on Leasing: An Effective New Legal Framework to Support Leasing Markets in the Developing Countries'. *Uniform Law Review* (2009): 637–647.

Tiberg, H. 'Power and Authority in the Law of Agency'. *Lex Mercatoria: Essays on International Commercial Law in Honour of Francis Reynolds*, edited by F.D. Rose. London: LLP, 2000.

Tzeng, C. *Ottawa-Konvention und nationales Recht: kollisionsrechtliche Probleme bei Anwendung der Ottawa-Konvention.* München: Utz, 2002, XXI–210 (*Münchner juristische Beiträge*, 27).

Factoring

A.M. & A. Zanotti (eds). *Developments in European, Italian and Israeli Law.* Milano: Giuffrè Editore, 2001 (*Seminario Giuridico della Università di Bologna, Miscellanee* 24).

Castro, R.A. de Oliveira *O factoring internacional no Brasil e na Argentina: una proposta de unificaçãon com base na Convençãon de Ottawa do UNIDROIT*. Tesi, Orientadora: Araminta de Azevedo Mercadante, São Paulo: Universidade de São Paulo, 2008, 397.

Dutrey Guantes, Y. *El Contrato Internacional De Factoring*. Madrid: Universidad Complutense Facultad de Derecho, Servicio de Publicaciones, 2000.

Ferrari, F. 'The International Sphere of Application of the 1988 Ottawa Convention on International Factoring'. *Developments in European, Italian and Israeli Law*, edited by A.M. Rabello. & A. Zanotti. Milano: Giuffrè Editore, 2001 (Seminario Giuridico della Università di Bologna, Miscellanee 24).

Goergen, U. *Das* Pactum de non cedendo. *Eine Untersuchung zum vertraglichen Abtretungsverbot im englischen, französischen und deutschen Recht unter Einbeziehung internationaler Harmonisierungsinitiativen.* Baden-Baden: Nomos Verlagsgesellschaft, 2000 (*Europäisches Privatrecht*, 13).

Hausler, C. 'Die Neuregelung der internationalen Forderungsfinanzierung durch das UNIDROIT-Übereinkommen über internationales Factoring'. *Handbuch des nationalen und internationalen Factoring*, 269. 3, völlig neu bearbeitete Auflage. Frankfurt am Main: Fritz Knapp Verlag, 1997.

Torsello, M. 'The Relationship Between the Parties to the Factoring Contract According to the 1988 UNIDROIT Convention on International Factoring [in English and in French]'. *Revue de droit des affaires internationales* (2000): 43–59.

Torsello, M. 'The Relationship Between the Parties to the Factoring Contract According to the 1988 UNIDROIT Convention on International Factoring'. *Developments in European, Italian and Israeli Law*, edited by A.M. Rabello. & A. Zanotti (Seminario Giuridico della Università di Bologna, Miscellanee 24), Milano: Giuffrè Editore, 2001.

International Interests in Mobile Equipment

(a) The Cape Town Convention

Atwood, J. 'The Status of the Mobile Equipment (Cape Town) Convention – Arrival of an International Registration System'. *Uniform Commercial Code Law Journal* 39 (2006): 1, 75–98.

Boliver, A. 'Square Pegs in a Round Hole? The Effects of the 2006 Cape Town Treaty Implementation and its Impact on Fractional Jet Ownership'. *Journal of Air Law and Commerce* 72 (2007): 529–560.

Bollweg, H.-G. & C. Henrichs. 'Das Übereinkommen von Kapstadt: Diplomatische Konferenz beschließt Übereinkünfte über Sicherungsrechte an Luftfahrtausrüstung'. *Zeitschrift für Luft- und Weltraumrecht* 51 (2002): 186–198.

Buckley, R. 'Overseas Law: Convention on International Interests in Mobile Equipment'. *Australian Law Journal* 75 (2001): 731–734.

Selected Bibliography

Burman, H.S. 'The Commercial Challenge in Modernizing Secured Transactions Law'. *Uniform Law Review* 8 (2003): 347–352.

Buxbaum, R.M. 'Montesquieu and the Cape Town Convention: of Bankruptcy and Civil Procedure'. *National, International, Transnational: Harmonischer Dreiklang im Recht*, 2020, pp. 733–742.

Chye, E. 'The Cape Town Convention – The Australian experience and views from the classroom'. *The University of Western Australia Law Review*, 40 (2016) 2, pp. 23–40.

Cuming, R. 'Overview of the Convention on International Interests in Mobile Equipment, 2001'. *Uniform Commercial Code Law Journal* 35 (2002): 73–86.

Cuming, R. 'The Characterisation of Interests and Transactions under the Convention of International Interests in Mobile Equipment, 2001'. *Security Interests in Mobile Equipment, Aldershot, Dartmouth Publishing Company*, edited by I. Burlington Davies. VT: Ashgate Publishing Limited, 2002.

Cuniberti, G. 'Advance Relief under the Cape Town Convention'. *Cape Town Convention Journal* (2012): 79–94.

Deschamps, M. 'Les règles de priorité de la Convention et du Protocol du Cap [in English and in French]'. *Uniform Law Review* 7 (2002): 17–48.

Deschamps, M. 'The perfection and priority rules of the Cape Town Convention and the Aircraft Protocol: a comparative analysis'. *Cape Town Convention Journal* (2013): 51–64.

Devaux, C. 'Le rôle des experts dans l'élaboration de la convention du Cap: entre autorité et légitimité'. *The future of transnational law*, 2015, pp. 427–457.

Didenko, A.N. 'The Cape Town Convention: a documentary history'. (*Hart Studies in Commercial and Financial Law* 5). Hart, 2021, pp. xxii-215.

Eshraghi Arani, M. 'The legal impediments to the accession of Iran to the Cape Town Convention on International Interests in Mobile Equipment and the Aircraft Protocol'. *Uniform Law Review*, 24 (2019) 1, pp. 234–253.

Foëx, B. 'La Convention du Cap relative aux garanties internationales portant sur des matériels d'équipement mobiles'. *La défaillance de paiement – Retard et défaut de paiement,* edited by B. Foëx. B. Fribourg: Editions universitaires, 2003.

Foëx, B. 'Les sûretés grevant les moyens de transport : la convention du Cap et sa transposition en droit national'. *Rapports suisses présentés au XIXe Congrès international de droit compare = Swiss reports presented at the XIXth international Congress of comparative law*, 2014, pp. 269–285.

Gao, S. & Fan, J. 'The latest international law on railway rolling stock finance and the respondence of China – Based on the Cape Town Convention and the Luxembourg Rail Protocol'. *Business and Economic Law Review*, (2019) 2, pp. 1–17.

Guerrero Lebrón, M.J. 'El convenio de Ciudad del Cabo: un registro electrónico internacional como paso previo a la armonización del régimen de la garantías mobiliarias'. *Derecho del sistema financiero y tecnología* (2010): 125–165.

Goode, R. 'The Cape Town Convention on International Interests in Mobile Equipment: A Driving Force for International Asset-based Financing'. *Uniform Law Review* 7 (2002): 3–15.

Goode, R. 'The Cape Town Convention on International Interests in Mobile Equipment: A Driving Force for International Asset-based Financing'. *Uniform Commercial Code Law Journal* (2003): 1–18.

Goode, R.M. 'The International Interest as an Autonomous Property Interest'. *European Review of Private Law* 12 (2004): 18–25.

Goode, R.M. 'The Priority Rules under the Cape Town Convention and Protocols'. *Cape Town Convention Journal* (2012): 95–108.

Goode, R.M. 'Asset Identification under the Cape Town Convention and Protocols'. *Law and Contemporary Problems* 81(1) (2018): 135–154.

Goode, R.M. 'Creativity and transnational commercial law: from Carchemish to Cape Town'. *International and Comparative Law Quarterly* 70 (2021) 1–28.

Goode, R.M. 'Issues of interpretation under the Cape Town Convention and its protocols' *Arbitrato, contratti e diritto del commercio internazionale.* 179–201.

Gullifer, L. 'A Comparison of the Position of Buyers under the Cape Town Convention, the Three Existing Protocols and the Draft MAC Protocol'. *Cape Town Convention Journal* 6 (2017): 97–121.

Honnebier, B.P. & J.M. Milo. 'The Convention of Cape Town: The Creation of International Interests in Mobile Equipment'. *European Review of Private Law* 12 (2004): 3–8.

Honnebier, B.P. 'De (internationale) leasing transactie als financieringsmethode van roerende kapitaalgoederen'. *Tijdschrift Onderneming en Financiering* 50 (April 2002): 59–69.

Honnebier, B.P. 'Een internationale uniforme materiële regeling voor het eigendomsvoorbehoud is tot stand gekomen. De conventie van Kaapstad'. *Tijdschrift voor Nederlands Burgerlijk Recht* 19 (2002): 233–238.

Honnebier, B.P. 'The Convention of Cape Town on International Interests in Mobile Equipment: The Solution of Specific European Property Law Problems'. *European Review of Private Law* 10 (2002): 377–395.

Honnebier, B.P. 'The Dutch Real Rights can be the Basis of International Interests under the Convention of Cape Town, Just Like Their Equivalent American Security Interests'. *European Review of Private Law* 12 (2004): 46–66.

Humphrey, N.& Nase, V. 'The Cape Town Convention 2001: An Australian Perspective'. *Air and space law* 31 (2006): 5–18.

Kozuka, S. 'The Legal System Conductive to Asset-Based Financing: Reflections on the Cape Town Convention on International Interests in Mobile Equipment [in Japanese]'. *Sophia Law Review* 46 no. 3 (2003), 43–78.

Kozuka, S. 'Security interests in transport vehicles: the Cape Town Convention and its implementation in national law'. *General Reports of the XIXth Congress of the International Academy of Comparative Law*, 2017, pp. 455–467.

Kozuka, S. 'The Cape Town Convention and the "Fitness" to the Context: Considering the Features of Aircraft, Rail and Space Financing'. *National, International, Transnational: Harmonischer Dreiklang im Recht*, 2020, pp. 1005–1015.

Kronke, H. 'Neues internationales Mobiliarsicherungsrecht erleichtert die Finanzierung von Luft- und Raumfahrzeugen: UNIDROIT-Konvention in Kapstadt verabschiedet'. *Zeitschrift für Luft- und Weltraumrecht* 51 (2002): 147–185.

Kronke, H. 'Parteiautonomie und Prorogationsfreiheit im internationalen Mobiliarsicherungsrecht: zwei Grundprinzipien der Konvention von Kapstadt'. *Liber Amicorum Gerhard Kegel*, edited by H. Krüger & H.P. Mansel. München: Beck, 2002.

Selected Bibliography

Laval, S. 'Pour une ratification de la Convention du Cap relative aux garanties internationales portant sur des matériels d'équipement mobiles. *Journal du droit international*, (2018) 4, doctr. 10.

Poulain, B. 'La Communauté européenne et la Convention du Cap'. *Uniform Law Review* 8 (2003): 377–386.

Pritchard, J. & Lloyd, D. 'Analysis of non-consensual rights and interests under Article 39 of the Cape Town Convention'. *Cape Town Convention Journal* (2013): 3–40.

Riffard, J.-F. 'La ratification de la Convention du Cap et de son Protocole ferroviaire: la délicate alchimie du choix des déclarations (ou du bon usage du sur-mesure d'un point de vue français)'. *Uniform Law Review*, 25 (2020) 1, pp. 92–108.

Rosen, H. 'Commentary on "A Comparison of the Position of Buyers under the Cape Town Convention, the Three Existing Protocols and the Draft MAC Protocol"'. *Cape Town Convention Journal* 6 (2017): 122–135.

Sagaert, V. 'The UNIDROIT Convention on International Interests in Mobile Equipment: A Belgian Perspective'. *European Review of Private Law* 12 (2004): 75–90.

Scott Wilson, F. 'Reflections on two Cape Town Convention innovations'. *Air & Space Lawyer* 31(1) (2018): 6–10.

Sester, P. & S. Haag. 'Die Umsetzung der Kapstadt-Konvention: Kollisionen mit dem deutschen Vollstreckungs-und Insolvenzrecht'. *Zeitschrift für Luft- und Weltraumrecht* 54 (2005): 493–512.

Stanford, M.J. 'From Ottawa to Cape Town: UNIDROIT's Role in the Modernisation of the Law Governing Leasing and the Taking of Security'. *Security Interests in Mobile Equipment*, edited by I. Davies. Aldershot: Dartmouth Publishing Company, Ashgate Publishing Limited, 2002.

Stanford, M.J. 'Cape Town Convention on International Interests in Mobile Equipment'. *World Leasing Yearbook* (2003): 35 et seq.

Stanford, M.J. 'International Law Reform: The UNIDROIT Leasing Convention and the Cape Town Convention'. *World Leasing Yearbook* (2004): 45 et seq.

Stanford, M.J. 'The New Regimen: Its History and Future after South Africa'. *European Review of Private Law* 12 (2004): 9–17.

The Guide on Best Practices in Electronic Collateral Registries (*Cape Town Convention Academic Project*), 2021. pp. X-69.

Thorne, P. & J. Edwards. 'The Cape Town Convention'. *Legal Flyer of the Norton Rose Aviation Group* 2 (2002): 2–4.

Traschler, T. 'The significance of the qualifying declarations under the Cape Town Convention'. *Uniform Law Review*, 24(1) (2019): 42–57.

Van Erp, S. 'The Cape Town Convention: A Model for a European System of Security Interests Registration?' *European Review of Private Law* 12 (2004): 91–110.

Wool, J. & Jonovic, A. 'The relationship between transnational commercial law treaties and national law: a framework as applied to the Cape Town Convention'. *Cape Town Convention Journal* (2013): 65–129.

(b) The Aircraft Protocol

Bodungen, B. von., *Mobiliarsicherungsrechte an Luftfahrzeugen und Eisenbahnrollmaterial im nationalen und internationalen Rechtsverkehr: zugleich ein Beitrag zur internationalen Vereinheitlichung des Rechtes nationaler Mobiliarsicherheiten durch das Kapstadt-Übereinkommen*, Münster et al.: Lit-Verl., 2009, XXIX-458. – (*Schriften zum europäischen Transport- und Verkehrsrecht*; 9).

Boliver, A. 'Square Pegs in a Round Hole? The Effects of the 2006 Cape Town Treaty Implementation and its Impact on Fractional Jet Ownership'. *Journal of Air Law and Commerce* 72 (2007): 529–560.

Cowan, R. 'Comparison of the Aircraft and MAC International Registries'. *Cape Town Convention Journal* 7 (2018): 21–37.

Cuming, R. 'The Registry System of the (Draft) Convention on International Interests in Mobile Equipment and the (Draft) Aircraft Equipment Protocol'. *Revue du Notariat* 103 (2001): 33–50.

Cuming, R.C.C. 'The International Registry for Interests in Aircraft: An Overview of its Structure'. *Uniform Law Review* 11 (2006): 18–59.

Deschamps, M. 'The perfection and priority rules of the Cape Town Convention and the Aircraft Protocol: a comparative analysis'. *Cape Town Convention Journal* (2013): 51–64.

Didenko, A.N. 'The Cape Town Convention: a documentary history'. (*Hart Studies in Commercial and Financial Law* 5). Hart, 2021, pp. xxii-215.

Eshraghi Arani, M. 'The legal impediments to the accession of Iran to the Cape Town Convention on International Interests in Mobile Equipment and the Aircraft Protocol'. *Uniform Law Review*, 24(1) (2019): 234–253.

Goode, R.M. *Convention on International Interests in Mobile Equipment and Protocol thereto on Matters Specific to Aircraft Equipment: Official commentary*; 3rd ed. Rome, UNIDROIT, 2013, pp. xviii-763; reprinted with corrections. Rome: UNIDROIT, 2016, pp. xviii-763.

Goode, R.M. *Convention on International Interests in Mobile Equipment and Protocol thereto on Matters Specific to Aircraft Equipment: Official Commentary*; 4th ed., Rome, UNIDROIT, 2019, pp. xxiii-833.

Goode, R.M. 'Convention on International Interests in Mobile Equipment and Protocol thereto on Matters Specific to Aircraft Objects: Official Commentary'. 5th ed. Rome UNIDROIT, 2022, pp. xxv-897.

Goode, R. Convention relative aux garanties internationales portant sur des matériels d'équipement mobiles et protocole y relatif portant sur les questions spécifiques aux matériels d'équipement aéronautiques. Commentaire officiel. Rome: Institut international pour l'unification du droit privé (UNIDROIT), 2002.

Goode, R.M. 'Creativity and transnational commercial law: from Carchemish to Cape Town'. *International and Comparative Law Quarterly* 70 (2021) 1–28.

Goode, R.M. 'Issues of interpretation under the Cape Town Convention and its protocols' *Arbitrato, contratti e diritto del commercio internazionale*. 179–201.

Gullifer, L. 'A Comparison of the Position of Buyers under the Cape Town Convention, the Three Existing Protocols and the Draft MAC Protocol'. *Cape Town Convention Journal* 6 (2017): 97–121.

Kozuka, S. 'The Cape Town Convention and the "Fitness" to the Context: Considering the Features of Aircraft, Rail and Space Financing'. *National, International, Transnational: Harmonischer Dreiklang im Recht*, 2020, pp. 1005–1015.

Kreuzer, K. 'Internationale Mobiliarsicherungsrechte an Luftfahrausrüstung. Zu der Convention on International Interests in Mobile Equipment und dem Protocol to the Convention on International Interests in Mobile Equipment on Matters specific to Aircraft Equipment'. *Festschrift für Peter Schlechtriem zum 70. Geburtstag*, edited by I. Schwenzer & G. Hager. Tübingen: J.B.C. Mohr (Paul Siebeck), 2003.

MacNally, M. *Recht der Sicherung und der Finanzierung von Luftfahrzeugen: unter besonderer Berücksichtigung des Übereinkommens über internationale Sicherungsrechte an beweglicher Ausrüstung und des Protokolls betreffend Besonderheiten der Luftfahrzeugausrüstung* (Kapstadt 2001), Zürich: Dike, 2009, XLII-284 (*Schriften zur Luftfahrt*; 3).

Mauri, G. 'La convenzione di Città del Capo e il protocollo aeronautico'. *Contratto e impresa* 14 (2009): 1, 503–522.

McPhillips, R. & Rosen, H. & Kozuka, S. & Kennedy, S. 'Comparative Analysis of Aircraft, Rail and Space International Registries and Their Regulatory Provisions'. *Cape Town Convention Journal* 5 (2016): 29–67.

Noël, L. 'La Convention du Cap relative aux garanties internationales portant sur des matériels d'équipement mobiles et le Protocole portant sur des questions spécifiques aux matériels d'équipement aéronautiques'. *ASDA Bulletin* (2003): 9–14.

Rosen, H. 'Commentary on "A Comparison of the Position of Buyers under the Cape Town Convention, the Three Existing Protocols and the Draft MAC Protocol"'. *Cape Town Convention Journal* 6 (2017): 122–135.

Sagaert, V. 'De UNIDROIT-Conventie betreffende internationale zakelijke rechten op roerend uitrustingsmaterieel: een laatste strohalm voor de belgische luchtvaartindustrie'. *Rechtskundig Weekblad* (2002): 1367–1369.

Salomons, A.F. 'Should We Ratify the Convention on International Interests in Mobile Equipment and the Air Equipment Protocol? Some Remarks from a Dutch Point of View'. *European Review of Private Law* 12 (2004): 67–74.

Standell, J.R. 'The Role of the International Registry Task force (I.R.T.F.) in the Development of the International Registry for Interests in Aircraft'. *Uniform Law Review*. 11 (2006): 8–17.

The Guide on Best Practices in Electronic Collateral Registries (*Cape Town Convention Academic Project*), 2021. pp. X-69.

Uniform Law Foundation, *Advanced Contract and Opinion Practices under the Cape Town Convention: The Legal Advisory Panel of the Aviation Working Group*. Oxford; Portland; Oregon: Hart publishing, 2008, X-66 (Cape Town papers series; 2).

Weber, L. 'The New Registry for International Interests in Aircraft Equipment under the Cape Town Convention and Protocol of 2001'. *Zeitschrift für Luft- und Weltraumrecht* 55 (2006): 1–21.

(c) The Rail Protocol

Bodungen, B. von., *Mobiliarsicherungsrechte an Luftfahrzeugen und Eisenbahnrollmaterial im nationalen und internationalen Rechtsverkehr: zugleich ein Beitrag zur internationalen Vereinheitlichung des Rechtes nationaler Mobiliarsicherheiten durch das Kapstadt-Übereinkommen*, Münster et al.: Lit-Verl., 2009, XXIX-458. – (*Schriften zum europäischen Transport- und Verkehrsrecht*; 9) – ISBN 978-3-82-581949-1.

Didenko, A.N. 'The Cape Town Convention: a documentary history'. (*Hart Studies in Commercial and Financial Law* 5). Hart, 2021, pp. xxii-215.

Gao, S. & Fan, J. 'The latest international law on railway rolling stock finance and the respondence of China – Based on the Cape Town Convention and the Luxembourg Rail Protocol'. *Business and Economic Law Review*, (2019) 2, pp. 1–17.

Goode, R.M. 'Convention on International Interests in Mobile Equipment and Luxembourg protocol thereto on matters specific to railway rolling stock: Official commentary'; 2nd ed., Rome, UNIDROIT, 2014, pp. xv-583.

Goode, R.M. 'Creativity and transnational commercial law: from Carchemish to Cape Town'. *International and Comparative Law Quarterly* 70 (2021) 1–28.

Goode, R.M. 'Issues of interpretation under the Cape Town convention and its protocols' *Arbitrato, contratti e diritto del commercio internazionale*. 179–201.

Gullifer, L. 'A Comparison of the Position of Buyers under the Cape Town Convention, the Three Existing Protocols and the Draft MAC Protocol'. *Cape Town Convention Journal*, 6 (2017): 97–121.

Kozuka, S. 'Rail Protocol to UNIDROIT's Mobile Equipment Convention and the Asset-Based Financing [in Japanese]'. *Journal of the Japan Overseas Rolling Stock Association* 217 (2003): 1–10.

Kozuka, S. 'The Cape Town Convention and the "Fitness" to the Context: Considering the Features of Aircraft, Rail and Space Financing'. *National, International, Transnational: Harmonischer Dreiklang im Recht*, 2020, pp. 1005–1015.

McPhillips, R. & Rosen, H. & Kozuka, S. & Kennedy, S. 'Comparative Analysis of Aircraft, Rail and Space International Registries and Their Regulatory Provisions'. *Cape Town Convention Journal* 5 (2016): 29–67.

Otabor-Olubor, I. 'Exporting the Luxembourg Rail Protocol to the Convention on International Interests in Mobile Equipment to Africa'. *Uniform Law Review,* 27 (2022) 1.

Riffard, J.-F. 'La ratification de la Convention du Cap et de son Protocole ferroviaire : la délicate alchimie du choix des déclarations (ou du bon usage du sur-mesure d'un point de vue français)'. *Uniform Law Review*, 25 (2020) 1, pp. 92–108.

Rosen, H. 'Building a Railway to the Future – Progress on the Draft UNIDROIT/OTIF Rail Protocol [in English and in French]'. *Uniform Law Review* (2001): 50–59.

Rosen, H. 'Les chemins de fer face aux enjeux de demain – État des travaux sur le projet de Protocole ferroviaire UNIDROIT/OTIF' [en français et en anglais]. *Uniform Law Review* (2001): 50–59.

Rosen, H. 'The Regimen of the Railway Rolling Stock Protocol'. *European Review of Private Law* 12 (2004): 26–36.

Stanford, M.J. 'UNIDROIT's Project for the Creation of a New International Regimen Governing the Taking of Security over High-value Mobile Equipment: A Window of Opportunity for the Financing of Railway Rolling Stock and Commercial Space Activities'. *Revista mexicana de derecho internacional privado y comparado* (2003): 91–150.

Rosen, H. 'Commentary on "A Comparison of the Position of Buyers under the Cape Town Convention, the Three Existing Protocols and the Draft MAC Protocol"'. *Cape Town Convention Journal* 6 (2017): 122–135.

The Guide on Best Practices in Electronic Collateral Registries (*Cape Town Convention Academic Project*), 2021. pp. X-69.

Von Bodungen, B. & Rosen, H. 'From the Luxembourg Rail Protocol to the draft MAC Protocol'. *Uniform Law Review* 23(2) (2018): 190–213.

Von Bodungen, B. & Rosen, H. 'From the Luxembourg Rail Protocol to the draft MAC Protocol'. *Uniform Law Review* 23(2) (2018): 190–213.

(d) The Space Protocol

Balsano, A.M. 'Modernising Secured Transactions Law: A Viewpoint from the European Space Agency'. *Uniform Law Review* 8 (2003): 375–376.

Bertrand, T. *Le financement des satellites et les sûretés réelles mobilières conventionnelles*. Mémoire pour l'obtention du Diplôme d'Étude Approfondie (DEA) de Droit International Public et Privé, sous la direction de M. le Professeur Louis Balmond. Nice, Université de Nice Sophia-Antipolis, Institut du droit de la paix et du développement (IDPD), 2000.

Didenko, A.N. 'The Cape Town Convention: a documentary history'. (*Hart Studies in Commercial and Financial Law* 5). Hart, 2021, pp. xxii-215.

Fenema, P. van. 'The UNIDROIT Space Protocol, the Concept of "Launching State", Space Traffic Management and the Delimitation of Outer Space. The 41st session of the UNCOPUOS Legal Subcommittee'. *Air & Space Law*. Vienna 2–12 April 2002, 27 (2002): 266–279.

Goode, R.M. *Convention on International Interests in Mobile Equipment and Protocol thereto on Matters Specific to Space Assets: Official Commentary* Rome, UNIDROIT, 2013, pp. xvi-653.

Goode, R.M. 'Creativity and transnational commercial law: from Carchemish to Cape Town'. *International and Comparative Law Quarterly* 70 (2021) 1–28.

Goode, R.M. 'Issues of interpretation under the Cape Town Convention and its protocols' *Arbitrato, contratti e diritto del commercio internazionale*. 179–201.

Gullifer, L. 'A Comparison of the Position of Buyers under the Cape Town Convention, the Three Existing Protocols and the Draft MAC Protocol'. *Cape Town Convention Journal* 6 (2017): 97–121.

Höpfli, M. *Rechtsrahmen für die wirtschaftliche Nutzung des Weltraumes durch Privatunternehmen: eine Analyse zentraler Rechtsfragen der wirtschaftlichen Nutzung des Weltraumes durch Privatunternehmen unter besonderer Berücksichtigung der Convention on International Interests in Mobile Equipment vom November 2001 in Verbindung mit dem UNIDROIT Preliminary Draft Protocol on Matters Specific to Space Assets vom Januar 2002*, Würzburg, 2003, 371. Universität Würzburg, Diss. 2002 (*Würzburger rechtswissenschaftliche Schriften*, 42).

Kozuka, S. 'The Commercialisation of the Space and the Legal Infrastructure for Asset-Based Financing: Commentary on the Draft Protocol on Space Assets to the Cape Town Convention (parts 1 & 2) [in Japanese]'. *Sophia Law Review* 46 no. 4 (2003), 1–20; 47, no. 1 (2003), 1–43.

Kozuka, S. 'The Cape Town Convention and the "Fitness" to the Context: Considering the Features of Aircraft, Rail and Space Financing'. *National, International, Transnational: Harmonischer Dreiklang im Recht*, 2020, pp. 1005–1015.

Kronke, H. 'The Draft UNIDROIT Convention on International Interests in Mobile Equipment and the Draft Protocol on Matters Specific to Space Assets'. *'Project 2001' – Legal Framework for the Commercial Use of Outer Space. Recommendations and Conclusions to Develop the Present State of the Law. Proceedings of an International Colloquium*, edited by K.-H. Böckstiegel. Cologne, May 29–31, 2001 to present Conclusions of 'Project 2001' – a joint International Research Project, Köln et al., Carl Heymanns Verlag, 2002, 643–656.

McPhillips, R. & Rosen, H. & Kozuka, S. & Kennedy, S. 'Comparative Analysis of Aircraft, Rail and Space International Registries and Their Regulatory Provisions'. *Cape Town Convention Journal* 5 (2016): 29–67.

Porras, D.A. 'Entering into force: promoting UNIDROIT's Space Protocol among emerging space actors'. *Implementing the Cape Town Convention and the domestic laws on secured transactions*, 2017.

Porras, D.A. 'The preliminary draft protocol to the Cape Town convention on matters specific to space assets'. *Convergence*, 5 (2009) 2, pp. 200–216.

Ribbelink, O.M. 'The Protocol on Matters Specific to Space Assets'. *European Review of Private Law* 12 (2004): 37–45.

Rosen, H. 'Commentary on "A Comparison of the Position of Buyers under the Cape Town Convention, the Three Existing Protocols and the Draft MAC Protocol"'. *Cape Town Convention Journal* 6 (2017): 122–135.

Stanford, M.J. & A. de Fontmichel. 'Overview of the Current Situation Regarding the Preliminary Draft Space Property Protocol and its Examination by COPUOs' [in English and French]. *Uniform Law Review* (2001): 60–77.

Sundahl, M.J. *The Cape Town Convention Its Application to Space Assets and Relation to the Law of Outer Space*, Leiden: Martinus Nijhoff Publishers, 2013, xiii-266.

Tăiatu, C.M. 'The International Telecommunication Union (ITU) as the proposed Supervisory Authority of the future International Registry for Space Assets'. *Uniform Law Review*, 23 (2018) 3/4, pp. 506–526.

The Guide on Best Practices in Electronic Collateral Registries (*Cape Town Convention Academic Project*), 2021. pp. X-69.

Weber-Steinhaus, D. & Ní Chearbhaill, D. 'Security Rights Over Satellites: An Overview of the Proposed Protocol to the Convention on International Interests in Mobile Equipment on Matters Specific to Space Assets'. *Contracting for Space* (2011), 221–231.

(e) The MAC Protocol

Cowan, R. 'Comparison of the Aircraft and MAC International Registries'. *Cape Town Convention Journal*, 7 (2018), pp. 21–37.

Selected Bibliography

Didenko, A.N. 'The Cape Town Convention: a documentary history'. (*Hart Studies in Commercial and Financial Law* 5). Hart, 2021, pp. xxii-215.

Dubovec, M. 'Accessions and Non-Accessions under the Cape Town Convention: Special Focus on MAC Equipment'. *Cape Town Convention Journal* 6 (2017): 52–65.

Durham, P.L. & Dubovec, M. 'More Good News from Cape Town: How the New MAC Protocol Will Benefit the Mining, Agriculture and Construction Industries'. *The Journal of Equipment Lease Financing* 35(1) (2017): 1–6.

Gabriel, H.D. 'The MAC Protocol: We Aren't There Yet – How Far Do We Have to Go'. *Cape Town Convention Journal* 4(1) (2015): 67–75.

Goode, R.M. *Convention on International Interests in Mobile Equipment and Protocol thereto on Matters Specific to Mining, Agricultural and Construction Equipment: Official Commentary*, Rome, UNIDROIT, 2021, pp. xxx-790.

Goode, R.M. 'Creativity and transnational commercial law: from Carchemish to Cape Town'. *International and Comparative Law Quarterly* 70 (2021) 1–28.

Goode, R.M. 'Issues of interpretation under the Cape Town Convention and its protocols' *Arbitrato, contratti e diritto del commercio internazionale*. 179–201.

Gullifer, L. 'A Comparison of the Position of Buyers under the Cape Town Convention, the Three Existing Protocols and the Draft MAC Protocol'. *Cape Town Convention Journal* 6 (2017): 97–121c.

Josipović, T. 'MAC Protocol and Croatian Registered Security Rights in Mining, Agricultural and Construction Equipment'. *National, International, Transnational: Harmonischer Dreiklang im Recht*, 2020, pp. 929–946.

Mooney, C.W. 'The MAC Protocol: Some Comments and a Challenge'. *Cape Town Convention Journal* 4(1) (2015): 76–82.

Mooney, C.W. & Dubovec, M. & Brydie-Watson, W. 'The mining, agricultural and construction equipment protocol to the Cape Town Convention project: The current status'. *Uniform Law Review* 21(2–3) (2016): 332–360.

Rodríguez de las Heras Ballell, T. 'Complexities arising from the expansion of the Cape Town Convention to other sectors: the MAC Protocol's challenges and innovative solutions'. *Uniform Law Review* 23(2) (2018): 214–241.

Rodríguez de las Heras Ballell, T. & Hara, M. 'MAC Protocol and Treaty Design: Examination of the Delimitation of Scope and Mechanism of Amendment'. *Cape Town Convention Journal* 6 (2017): 10–36.

Rosen, H. 'Commentary on "A Comparison of the Position of Buyers under the Cape Town Convention, the Three Existing Protocols and the Draft MAC Protocol"'. *Cape Town Convention Journal* 6 (2017): 122–135.

The Guide on Best Practices in Electronic Collateral Registries (*Cape Town Convention Academic Project*), 2021. pp. X-69.

Von Bodungen, B. & Mooney, C.W. 'Immovable-Associated Equipment under the Draft Mac Protocol: A Sui Generis Challenge for the Cape Town Convention'. *Cape Town Convention Journal* 6 (2017): 37–51.

Von Bodungen, B. & Rosen, H. 'From the Luxembourg Rail Protocol to the Draft MAC Protocol'. *Uniform Law Review* 23(2) (2018): 190–213.

Von Bodungen, B. & Rosen, H. 'From the Luxembourg Rail Protocol to the Draft MAC Protocol'. *Uniform Law Review*, 23(2) (2018): 190–213.

Wang, L. 'MAC protocol and the reform of the law of secured transaction in China'. *Business and Economic Law Review*, (2019) 2, pp. 33–48.

Warwick Economics and Associates & International Institute for the Unification of Private Law, *MAC Protocol Economic Assessment*, Rome, UNIDROIT, August 2018.

Franchising

Binder, O. 'Les Initiatives d'UNIDROIT en matière de franchisage: vers un système moderne et plus transparent de distribution des marchandises et des services'. *Uniform Law Review* (2000): 707–716.

Fernlund, A. 'Harmonised Legislation on Franchise Disclosure and National Law: The Case of Sweden'. *Uniform Law Review* (2000): 737–749.

Handa, Y. 'Franchisor no Joho Teikyo Gimu'. *Hogaku Ronshu* 20 (2005): 1–92.

International Institute for the Unification of Private Law (UNIDROIT), *Guide to International Master Franchise Arrangements*, 2nd edn. Rome: International Institute for the Unification of Private Law, 2007.

Kozuka, S. 'Franchise Keiyaku ni Kansuru UNIDROIT no modeluho souan [UNIDROIT's Draft Model Law on Franchising]', *NBL* (2001), No. 708, 6–11; No. 710, 30–37; No. 712, 66–74.

Kozuka, S. 'UNIDROIT No Franchise Kaijigimu Model Nô [UNIDROIT Franchise Model Disclosure Law]'. *Journal of the Japanese Institute of International Business Law* 30 (2002): 1189–1195; 1367–1372.

Kozuka, S. 'UNIDROIT No Franchise Kaijigimu Model Nô'. *Journal of the Japanese Institute of International Business Law* 30 (2002): 1189–1195, 1367–1372.

Kozuka, S. 'Overview of the Draft Model Law of UNIDROIT on Franchising'. *Tokyo Internet Law Journal*. <www.tokyointernetlawjournal.com/ronbun/UNIDROIT ModelLaw.PDF>.

Peters, L. 'The Draft UNIDROIT Model Franchise Disclosure Law and the Move Towards National Legislation'. *Uniform Law Review* (2000): 717–735.

Peters, L. 'UNIDROIT: Proposal for a Model Law on Franchising'. *International Business Lawyer* 28 (2000): 180–181.

Peters, L. 'UNIDROIT Prepares a Model Franchise Disclosure Law'. *Business Law International* (2000): 279–293.

Peters, L. 'Franchising: The UNIDROIT Guide to International Master Franchise Arrangements, The Draft Model Franchise Disclosure Law and Mexico'. *Revista Mexicana de Derecho Internacional Privado* (2001): 9, 69–94.

Peters, L. 'Il progetto preliminare di Legge modello UNIDROIT sull'informazione dovuta (disclosure) negli accordi di franchising'. *Franchising: Legislazione e pratica [Atti del Convegno 'Franchising: Legislazione e pratica – Presente e futuro' organizzato dall'Istituto Internazionale per l'Unificazione del Diritto Privato (UNIDROIT) e dalla Promofranchising – FIF Confesercenti*, Roma, 25 novembre 2000], 83–99. Roma: FIF Confesercenti, 2001.

Peters, L. 'The Draft UNIDROIT Model Law: Genesis and Contents'. *Franchising im Europäischen Privatrecht*, edited by R. Schulze (Hrsg.). Baden-Baden: Nomos Verlagsgesellschaft, 2001 (*Europäisches Privatrecht*, Band 18).

Peters, L. 'Una legge per il franchising'. *Diritto del Commercio Internazionale* 18 (2004): 323–334.

Peters, L. 'Genesis of a Model Law: the UNIDROIT Model Franchise Disclosure Law and Genesis its sources of inspiration'. *Uniform Law Review 2015*, pp. 81–115.

Scott, A. 'UNIDROIT's Model Franchise Disclosure Law Proposal'. *International Franchising* 5 (2001): 5.

Vernon, J. 'UNIDROIT Model Franchise Law'. *International Bar Association. Committee X News. Newsletter of the International Franchising Committee of the Section on Business Law* 6, no. 2 (2002): 11–12.

Zumbo, F. 'International Master Franchise Agreements'. *New Zealand Law Journal* (2000): 121–124.

Zumbo, F. 'UNIDROIT and International Franchising'. *Business Law Review* (2000): 16–17.

Transactions on Transnational and Related Capital Markets

Conac, P.-H. & Segna, U. & Thévenoz, L. (eds.) *Intermediated securities: the impact of the Geneva Securities Convention and the future European legislation*, Cambridge University Press, 2013, pp. XXX-406.

Institut International pour l'Unification du droit privé – Kanda, H. & Mooney, C. & Thévenoz, L. & Béraud, S. avec l'assistance de Keijser, Th. *Commentaire officiel de la convention d'UNIDROIT sur les règles matérielles relatives aux titres intermédiés: Convention de Genève sur les titres*. Schulthess Médias Juridiques: Genève; Zurich; Bâle, 2012, pp. 402. (*Publications du Centre de droit bancaire et financier*).

International Institute for the Unification of Private Law – Kanda, H. & Mooney, C. & Thévenoz, L. & Béraud, S. with the assistance of Keijser, Th. *Official Commentary on the UNIDROIT Convention on Substantive Rules for Intermediated Securities*. Oxford University Press, Oxford 2012, pp. xvii + 297.

Kronke, H. 'Connected and Global Securities Markets: With or Without Conflict of Laws?'. *Corporations, Capital Markets and Business in the Law. Liber Amicorum Richard M. Buxbaum*, edited by T. Baums, K.J. Hopt & N. Horn. The Hague: Kluwer Law International, 2000.

Kronke, H. 'Capital Markets and Conflict of Laws'. *Recueil des Cours de l'Académie de droit international* (2000): Tome 286. The Hague: Martinus Nijhoff Publishers, 2001.

Kronke, H. 'Entwicklungen des internationalen Kapitalmarktrechts und Schiedsgerichtsbarkeit'. *Law of International Business and Dispute Settlement in the 21st Century / Recht der Internationalen Wirtschaft und Streiterledigung im 21. Jahrhundert – Liber Amicorum Karl-Heinz Böckstiegel*, edited by R. Briner et al. Köln: Carl Heymanns Verlag, 2001.

Kronke, H. 'The Draft UNIDROIT Convention on Intermediate Securities: Transnational Certainty and Market Stability'. *Current Developments in Monetary and Financial Law* 5 (2008): 619–639.

Schwarcz, S.L. 'Indirectly Held Securities and Intermediary Risk'. *Uniform Law Review* 6 (2001): 283–300.

Vauplane, H. de. 'Projet de Convention UNIDROIT sur les règles de droit matériel applicables aux titres intermediès'. *Revue trimestrielle de droit financier* 2 (2006): 65–67.

Civil Procedure

(a) ALI/UNIDROIT Principles of Transnational Civil Procedure

(anon) *European Journal of Law Reform*, 4 (2002), Issue 1: Special Issue on the Future of International Civil Procedure, 250.

American Law Institute – International Institute for the Unification of Law, *Principles of transnational civil procedure: as adopted and promulgated by The American Law Institute at Washington, D.C., U.S.A. May 2004 and by UNIDROIT at Rome, Italy April 2004*, New York: Cambridge University Press, 2006, LIX-177.

Beaumont, B. 'The Proposed ALI/UNIDROIT Principles of Transnational Civil Procedure and Their Relationship to Australian jurisdictions'. *Uniform Law Review* 6 (2001): 951–970.

Béraudo, J.P. 'Réflexions sur les Principes ALI/UNIDROIT à propos de la preuve'. *Uniform Law Review* 6 (2001): 925–930.

Cadiet, L. 'The ALI–UNIDROIT project: from transnational principles to European rules of civil procedure: public conference, opening session, 18 October 2013'. *Uniform Law Review*, 19 (2014) 2, pp. 292–294.

Cooper, E.H. 'Transnational Civil Procedure: Fact Pleading or Notice Pleading? A viewpoint from the USA'. *Uniform Law Review* 6 (2001): 857–869.

Elmer, M.B. 'Brief considerations on the harmonisation of civil procedure in Europe and worldwide', *Uniform Law Review*, 8 (2003) 1/2, 461–463.

Elsen, S.H. 'An American Lawyer Looks At Litigation under the Proposed ALI/UNIDROIT Principles and Rules of Transnational Civil Procedure'. *Uniform Law Review* 6 (2001): 971–980.

Ferrand, F. 'Les "Principes" relatifs à la procédure civile transnationale sont-ils autosuffisants? – de la nécessité ou non de les assortir de 'Règles' dans le projet'. *Uniform Law Review* 6 (2001): 995–1013.

Ferrand, F. 'Les Principes ALI/UNIDROIT de procédure civile pour les litiges transnationaux en matière commerciale'. *Revue de droit des affaires internationales* (2006): 21–36.

Forner i Delaygua, J.J. 'El proyecto del American Law Institute transnational rules of civil procedure: la cooperación judicial', *Anuario español de derecho internacional privado*, 2000, 275–284.

Fouchard, P. (ed.). *Vers un procès civil universel? Les règles transnationales de procédure civile de l'American Law Institute [Colloque organisé par l'École doctorale de droit international, droit européen, relations internationales et droit comparé de l'Université Panthéon-Assas (Paris II le 27) octobre 2000*]. Paris: Editions Panthéon-Assas, 2001.

Fouchard, P. 'Une procédure civile transnationale: quelle fin et quels moyens?'. *Uniform Law Review* 6 (2001): 779–788.

Ghamami, M. & Hassan M. 'Principes ALI/UNIDROIT de procédure civile transnationale: étude comparée' Téhéran: Mizan, 2007.

Gidi, A. 'A presentação das normas trasnacionais de processo civil'. *Roma e America. Diritto Romano Comune. Rivista di Diritto dell'Integrazione e Unificazione del Diritto in Europa e in America Latina* 9 (2000): 335–345.

Gidi, A. 'Iniciativas para la formulación de normas uniformes en el ámbito del derecho procesal civil internacional'. *Derecho-PUC [Revista de la Facultad de Derecho de la Pontificia Universidad Católica del Perú]* (Diciembre 2001).

Gidi, A. 'Notes on Criticizing the Proposed ALI/UNIDROIT Principles and Rules of Transnational Civil Procedure'. *Uniform Law Review* 6 (2001): 819–826.

Glenn, H.P. 'The ALI/UNIDROIT Principles of Transnational Civil Procedure as Global Standards for Adjudication?'. *DeCITA* 4 (2005): 26–44.

Goldstein, S. 'The Proposed ALI/UNIDROIT Principles and Rules of Transnational Civil Procedure: The Utility of Such a Harmonization Project [in English and French]'. *Uniform Law Review* 6 (2001): 789–801.

Hazard, G.C. Jr. 'Transnational Rules of Civil Procedure: A Challenge to Judges and Lawyers'. *Studi Urbinati di Scienze Giuridiche, Politiche ed Economiche* 68 (1999/2000): 247–266.

Hazard, G.C. Jr. 'Transnational of Civil Procedure'. *Uniform Law Review* 6 (2001): 753–762.

Hazard, G.C. Jr., M. Taruffo, R. Stürner & A. Gidi. 'Normas del proceso civil transnacional'. *Derecho-PUC [Revista de la Facultad de Derecho de la Pontificia Universidad Católica del Perú]* (Diciembre 2001), No. 54, 263–287.

Kemelmajer De Carlucci, A. 'La charge de la preuve dans les Principes et Règles ALI/UNIDROIT relatifs à la procédure civile internationale'. *Uniform Law Review* 6 (2001): 915–924.

Kemelmajer de Carlucci, A. 'Lineamientos generales de los principios y reglas comunes para los procesos transnacionales (ALI/UNIDROIT)'. *DeCITA* 4 (2005): 45–60.

Kronke, H. 'Taking of Evidence under the UNIDROIT/American Law Institute Project "Transnational Principles of Civil Procedure"'. *Stockholm Arbitration Report* (2000): 1, 63–72.

Kronke, H. 'Efficiency, Fairness, Macro-economic functions: Challenges for the Harmonisation of Transnational Civil Procedure [in English and in French]'. *Uniform Law Review* 6 (2001): 740–751.

Kronke, H. 'Der Beweis im UNIDROIT/ALI-Projekt Transnational Principles of Civil Procedure'. *Beweiserhebung in internationalen Schiedsverfahren*, 2001, 77–83.

Mecarelli, G. 'Quelques réflexions en matière de discovery'. *Uniform Law Review* 6 (2001): 901–914.

Mestre, F. 'La armonización del proceso civil internacional: los principios y reglas elaborados por ALI-UNIDROIT'. *DeCITA* 3 (2005): 407–413.

Mikelénas, V. 'The Proposed ALI/UNIDROIT Principles and Rules of Transnational Civil Procedure and the New Code of Civil Procedure in Lithuania'. *Uniform Law Review* 6 (2001): 981–993.

Pfieffer, T. 'The ALI/UNIDROIT Project: Are Principles Sufficient, Without the Rules?' *Uniform Law Review* 6 (2001): 1015–1033.

Pour-Ostad, M. Principles of transnational civil procedure / Translated by Majid Pour-Ostad. – Teheran: S.D.I.L., 2008, pag. var..

Priestley, L.J. 'Transnational Civil Procedure – *Fact Pleading v. Notice Pleading*: Its Significance in the Development of Evidence'. *Uniform Law Review* 6 (2001): 841–855.

Principles of transnational civil procedure: as adopted and promulgated by The American Law Institute at Washington, D.C., U.S.A. May 2004 and by UNIDROIT at Rome, Italy April 2004. – New York, NY: Cambridge University Press, 2006. – pp. LIX-177.

Retornaz, V. 'La procédure de discovery of documents dans les règles et principes ALI/UNIDROIT de procédure civile transnationale: réflexions microscopiques sur l'harmonisation des lois de procédure civile', edited by C. Chappuis. *L'harmonisation internationale du droit*, 2007, 553–576.

Schack, H. 'Transnational Service of Process: A Call for Uniform and Mandatory Rules'. *Uniform Law Review* 6 (2001): 827–839.

Storme, M. 'Procedural Law and the Reform of Justice: From Regional to Universal Harmonisation'. *Uniform Law Review* 6 (2001): 763–777.

Stürner, R. 'Règles transnationales de procédure civile? Quelques remarques d'un Européen sur un nouveau projet commun de l'American Law Institute et d'UNIDROIT'. *Revue internationale de droit comparé* 52 (2000): 845–865.

Stürner, R. 'Some Remarks on a New Joint Project of the American Law Institute and UNIDROIT'. *The International Lawyer* 3 (2000): 1071–1086.

Stürner, R. 'Transnational Civil Procedure: Discovery and Sanctions Against Non-compliance'. *Uniform Law Review* 6 (2001): 871–886.

Stürner, R. 'The Principles of transnational civil procedure: an introduction to their basic conception'. *Rabels Zeitschrift für ausländisches und internationales Privatrecht*, 69 (2005), 201–254.

Sumampouw, M. 'Parental Responsibility under Brussels II'. *Private Law in the International Arena. From National Conflict Rules Towards Harmonization and Unification. Liber Amicorum Kurt Siehr.* Zürich: T.M.C. Asser Press, Schulthess, 2000.

Taruffo, M. 'A Project of Rules for Transnational Litigation'. *The Unification of International Commercial Law*. Baden-Baden: Nomos Verlagsgesellschaft, (1998), 189–199.

Voulgaris, I. [Trad.] – Αρχές ALI/UNIDROIT πολιτικής δικονομίας διακρατικού χαρακτήρα, *ΕΕμπΔ: Επιθεωρησις του Εμπορικου Δικαιου*, 3 (2016), 738–757.

Vrellis, S. 'Un juriste grec face au projet de procédure civile transnationale d'ALI/UNIDROIT'. *Le droit international privé* (2005): 817–829.

Walder, H.U. 'Die Principles and Rules of Transnational Civil Procedure im Lichte des schweizerischen Zivilprozessrechts'. *Privatrecht und Methode*, 2004, 1051–1063.

Walker, J. 'The Utility of the ALI/UNIDROIT Project on Principles and Rules of Transnational Civil Procedure'. *Uniform Law Review* 6 (2001): 803–818.

Waterstraat, D. 'ALI – UNIDROIT Principles and Rules of Transnational Civil Procedure: ein Instrument zur Lösung des deutsch-amerikanischen Justizkonflikts bei grenzüberschreitenden Beweisaufnahmen?'. 1. Aufl., Baden-Baden: Nomos, 2006, 211 (*Schriften des Augsburg Center for Global Economic Law and Regulation*; 4).

(b) ELI/UNIDROIT Model European Rules of Civil Procedure

Andrews, N. 'Fundamentals of costs law: loser responsibility, access to justice, and procedural discipline', *Uniform Law Review*, 19 (2014) 2, 295–307.

Selected Bibliography

Cadiet, L. 'The ALI–UNIDROIT project: from transnational principles to European rules of civil procedure'. *Uniform Law Review* 2014, 292–294.

ELI-UNIDROIT first exploratory workshop: from transnational principles to European rules of civil procedure / from the editorial board, *Uniform Law Review*, 19 (2014) 2, 171–172.

Gascón Inchausti, F., Stürner, M., 'Access to information and evidence in the ELI/UNIDROIT European rules on civil procedure: some fundamental aspects', *Uniform Law Review*, 24 (2019) 1, 14–41.

Hazard, G.C. Jr., 'Some preliminary observations on the proposed ELI-UNIDROIT civil procedure project in the light of the experience of the ALI–UNIDROIT project'. *Uniform Law Review*, 19 (2014) 2, pp. 176–178.

Jeuland, E., Smith, V., Stadler, A. [eds.], 'Collective and mass litigation in Europe: model rules for effective dispute resolution'. Edward Elgar, 2020. - xv-381.

Kramer, X.E. 'The structure of civil proceedings and why it matters: exploratory observations on future ELI-UNIDROIT European rules of civil procedure'. *Uniform Law Review*, 19 (2014) 2, pp. 218–238.

Trocker, N. 'From ALI–UNIDROIT Principles to common European rules on access to information and evidence?: a preliminary outlook and some suggestions'. *Uniform Law Review*, 19 (2014) 2, pp. 239–291.

UNIDROIT Principles and Rules of Transnational Civil Procedure: ein Instrument zur Lösung des deutsch-amerikanischen Justizkonflikts bei grenzüberschreitenden Beweisaufnahmen?'. 1. Aufl., Baden-Baden: Nomos, 2006, 211 (*Schriften des Augsburg Center for Global Economic Law and Regulation*; 4).Pfeiffer, T. 'The contribution of arbitration to the harmonization of procedural laws in Europe', *Uniform Law Review*, 2014, 199–217.

Prechal, S., Cath, K. 'The European acquis of civil procedure: constitutional aspects, *Uniform Law Review*, 2014, 179–198.

Storskrubb, E. 'Due notice of proceedings: present and future', Uniform Law Review, 2014, 351–364.

Stürner, R. 'Principles of European civil procedure or a European model code?: Some considerations on the joint ELI-UNIDROIT project'. *Uniform Law Review*, 19 (2014) 2, pp. 322–328.

Trocker, N. 'From ALI–UNIDROIT Principles to common European rules on access to information and evidence? A preliminary outlook and some suggestions', *Uniform Law Review*, 2014, 239–291.

Tzankova, I.N. 'Case management: the stepchild of mass claim dispute resolution', *Uniform Law Review*, 2014, 329–350.

Wallis, D. 'Introductory remarks on the ELI-UNIDROIT project'. *Uniform Law Review*, 19 (2014) 2, 173–175.

International Carriage of Goods by Road (CMR)

Alessandri, M. 'A General Overview on the Italian Case Law Regarding the Application of the Convention on the Contract for the International Carriage of Goods by Road (CMR)'. *Transportrecht* 28 (2005): 465–468.

Blom, A. 'The Necessity of the Operation of a "Casualty" During the Period of Cargo Insurance [Belgisch-Nederlands CMR-Seminar, 26 mei 2000]'. *European Transport Law* 35 (2000–3): 375–379.

Boggio, L. 'Il trasporto di merci su strada tra CMR e Convenzione di Roma (sulla legge applicabile alle obbligazioni contrattuali). [Note:] Corte d'Appello di Trieste 5 novembre 2001 (*Autamarocchi S.P.A. v. Alpina Versicherung AG*)'. *Il Diritto Marittimo* 104 (2002): 978–983.

Boggio, L. 'La C.M.R. in Cassazione: errare umanum est...'. *Diritto Marittimo* 102 (2000): 132–134.

Buyl, P. 'Artikel 23 §4 van het CMR-Verdrag getoetst aan de Algemene CMR-Verzekeringsvoorwaarden of de verbazing van de struisvogel [Belgisch-Nederlands CMR-Seminar, 26 mei 2000]'. *European Transport Law* 35 (2000–3): 343–349.

Clarke, M.A. *International Carriage of Goods by Road: CMR*. London: Sweet & Maxwell, 1997.

Clarke, M.A. *International Carriage of Goods by Road: CMR*. 5th edn. London: Informa, 2009, liv-514 (Lloyd's Transport Law Library).

Concepción, J.L. 'El dolo como causa de inaplicación del límite de responsabilidad: el articulo 29 de la Convención CMR. *Actualidad jurídica del transporte por carretera: in memoriam F.M. Sánchez Gamborino*. Madrid: Fundación Francisco Corell, 2005, 445–451.

Cornette, M. 'CMR – Uninsured liabilities and risks [Belgisch-Nederlands CMR-Seminar, 26 mei 2000]'. *European Transport Law* 35 (2000–3): 363–370.

Csoklich, P.H. 'Las reglas CMR como derecho aplicable al transporte nacional: la favorable experiencia de Austria'. *Actualidad jurídica del transporte por carretera: in memoriam F.M. Sánchez Gamborino*. Madrid: Fundación Francisco Corell, 2005.

Czapski, W. 'El concepto de transportista segun la convención CMR y la jurisprudencia'. *Actualidad jurídica del transporte por carretera: in memoriam F.M. Sánchez Gamborino*. Madrid: Fundación Francisco Corell, 2005.

Dißars, B.-A. 'Das Verhältnis der Zuständigkeitsnormen der CMR zum EuGVÜ/LugÜ'. *Transportrecht* 24 (2001): 387–393.

Djoric, A. *Le contrat de transport international terrestre des marchandises*. Institut za Uporedno Pravo; Ambassade de France en Serbie et Montenegro. Beograd: Cigoja (2005): 250.

Emparanza Sobejano, A. 'El transporte sucesivo en el convenio CMR, arts. 34 a 40: un modelo agotado'. *Actualidad jurídica del transporte por carretera: in memoriam F.M. Sánchez Gamborino*. Madrid: Fundación Francisco Corell (2005): 465–474.

Geuens, P. 'De elektronische CMR-vrachtbrief'. *Liber Amicorum Robert Wijffels*, edited by M.-P. Serck. Antwerpen: ETL, 2001.

Haak, K.F. 'De onstuitbare opmars van de CMR [Belgisch-Nederlands CMR-Seminar, 26 mei 2000]'. *European Transport Law* 35 (2000–3): 307–311.

Haak, K.F. 'CMR-Übereinkommen: Vertrag zu Lasten Dritter?'. Schachtschneider, K.A., Piper, H. & M. Hübsch (ed.), *Transport – Wirtschaft – Recht. Gedächtnisschrift für Johann Georg Helm*, 91–98. Berlin: Duncker & Humblot, 2001 (*Schriften zum Wirtschaftsrecht*, 133).

Haak, K.F. 'Revision der CMR?'. *Transportrecht* (2006): 325–336.

Haubold, J. 'CMR und europäisches Zivilverfahrensrecht: Klarstellungen zu internationaler Zuständigkeit und Rechtshängigkeit'. *IPRax* 26 (2006): 224–229.

Hemmes, J.E.J. 'El art. 3 de la convención CMR: un caso concreto de responsabilidad del transportista, que resulta ser el más habitual'. *Actualidad jurídica del transporte por carretera: in memoriam F.M. Sánchez Gamborino*. Madrid: Fundación Francisco Corell, 2005.

Heuer, K. 'CMR und EuGVÜ: Nochmals zur Frage der internationalen Zuständigkeit (Art. 31 Abs. 1 CMR/Art. 20 EuGVÜ) und zur Einrede der Rechtshängigkeit bei negativer Feststellungsklage (Art. 31 Abs. 2 CMR/Art. 21 EuGVÜ)'. *Transportrecht* 25 (2002): 221–225.

Heuer, K. 'Zur außervertraglichen Haftung des Frachtführers (und seines Kfz-Haftpflichtversicherers) für Güterfolgeschäden. Anmerkung zu Thume, VersR 2002, 267 ff'. *Transportrecht* 25 (2002): 325–326.

Johansson, S.O. 'The Scope and the Liability of the CMR – Is There a Need of Changes?'. *Transportrecht* 25 (2002): 385–392.

Knefel, A.O.E. 'From CMR to logistics [Belgisch-Nederlands CMR-Seminar, 26 mei 2000]'. *European Transport Law* 35 (2000–3): 371–374.

Koller, I. 'Übereinkommen über den Beförderungsvertrag im internationalen Straßengüterverkehr (CMR)'. *Transportrecht. Kommentar zu Spedition und Gütertransport*, edited by I. Koller. (4. völlig neubearbeitete Auflage) München: C.H. Beck'sche Verlagsbuchhandlung, 2000.

Koller, I. 'Gehilfen des CMR-Frachtführers und Art. 31 CMR'. *Transportrecht* 25 (2002): 133–136.

Laurijssen, P. 'Water en Weg – Botsing van wetten Stapelvervoer onder artikel 2 CMR'. *European Transport Law* 36 (2001): 799–826.

Loewe, R. 'La CMR y sus apóstoles'. *Actualidad jurídica del transporte por carretera: in memoriam F.M. Sánchez Gamborino*. Madrid: Fundación Francisco Corell, 2005.

Loyens, J. 'Zijn douanerechten, accijnzen, enz. kosten ten laste van de CMRvervoerder krachtens art. 23.4 CMR? [Belgisch-Nederlands CMR-Seminar, 26 mei 2000]'. *European Transport Law* 35 (2000–3): 351–361.

Mercadal, B. 'La carta de porte CMR según la jurisprudencia francesa y otros países'. *Actualidad jurídica del transporte por carretera: in memoriam F.M. Sánchez Gamborino*. Madrid: Fundación Francisco Corell, 2005.

Morán Bovio, D. 'El concepto de dolo y culpa equiparable a dolo por parte del transportista: art. 29 del convenio CMR'. *Actualidad jurídica del transporte por carretera: in memoriam F.M. Sánchez Gamborino*. Madrid: Fundación Francisco Corell, 2005.

Morandi, F. 'La limitazione dell'obbligazione risarcitoria del vettore stradale di cose per ritardo nel sistema di diritto uniforme'. *Trasporti* 65 (1995): 53.

Ondrej, J. 'Smlouvy o mezinárodní preprave se zamerením na Úmluvu o prepravní smlouve v mezinárodní silnicní nákladní doprave a její prováde a její provádení v právu CR', in: *Liber Amicorum Monika Pauknerova*, Prague, 2021, 309–317.

Ortiz Pavía, J.L. 'La responsabilidad del transportista, en el transporte internacional de mercancías por carretera: arts. 17 y sigientes del Convenio CMR'. *Actualidad jurídica del transporte por carretera: in memoriam F.M. Sánchez Gamborino*. Madrid: Fundación Francisco Corell, 2005.

Panopoulos, G. 'La jurisprudence grecque en matière de Conventions internationales relatives aux transports terrestres et aériens'. *Uniform Law Review* 9 (2004): 625–643.

Plasil, F. & Kliment, L. 'The CMR convention, Brussels I regulation and "Empty International Competence": the determination of territorial jurisdiction of national courts in disputes arising out of the international carriage of goods'. *International transportation*, 2015, pp. 169–186.

Putzeys, J. 'El transporte nacional de mercancias por carretera en Bélgica, bajo las reglas CMR: una experiencia positiva'. *Actualidad jurídica del transporte por carretera: in memoriam F.M. Sánchez Gamborino*. Madrid: Fundación Francisco Corell, 2005.

Putzeys, J. 'Preparation of a Protocol Additional to the CMR Concerning the Electronic Consignment Note'. *Uniform Law Review* 10 (2005): 532–535.

Putzeys, J. '*RR versus CMR?* In Free on Board'. *Liber amicorum Marc A. Huybrechts*, 2011, 469–484.

Ramberg, J. 'Los transportes por superposición (camión sobre tren o buque): el art. 2 del Convenio CMR en el contexto de la logistica del transporte'. *Actualidad jurídica del transporte por carretera: in memoriam F.M. Sánchez Gamborino*. Madrid: Fundación Francisco Corell, 2005.

Rogov, S. 'Anmerkung zu der bei der U.N.O. aufliegenden Übersetzung der CMR in die russische Sprache'. *European Transport Law* 36 (2001): 659–682.

Rogov, S. 'Ist die Russische Federation ein Vertragsstaat der CMR?'. *Transportrecht* 25 (2002): 62–64.

Rogov, S. 'Paradoxen der dualen Haftungsobergrenze des Art. 23 Abs. 3 CMR'. *Transportrecht* (2002): 286–289.

Rogov, S. 'Paradoxen der dualer Haftungsobergrenze des Art. 23 Abs. 3 CMR'. *European Transport Law* 37 (2002): 291–299.

Rosello, C. 'Tre questioni in tema di CMR: i presupposti di applicabilità della Convenzione; il regime dei trasporti misti o "sovrapposti"; la distribuzione dell'onere della prova relativa alla responsabilità del vettore'. *Diritto Marittimo* 54 (2002): 568–577.

Rüfner, T. 'Lis alibi pendens under the CMR – *Merzario v. Leitner*'. *Lloyd's Maritime and Commercial Law Quarterly* (2001): 460–465.

Ruitinga, P. & R.J. de Haan. 'Gabriële Wehr Revisited (The Results of Indulging in Fiction When Dealing with Statutes, Conventions or Legal Precedents Are Not Always Fortunate). Some Notes on Article 2 CMR'. *European Transport Law* 36 (2001): 831–842.

Sanchez Gamborino, F.J. *CMR Manual Práctico*. Madrid: Fundación Francisco Corell, 2000.

Sanchez Gamborino, F.J. 'La Convención CMR según la Jurisprudencia del "Tribunal Supremo" de España'. *European Transport Law* 36 (2001): 843–877.

Sanchez Gamborino, F.J. 'La jurisprudence du Tribunal Supremo espagnol en matière de CMR'. *Uniform Law Review* 6 (2001): 643–648.

Sanchez Gamborino, F.J. 'La CMR en tant que loi applicable au transport national'. *Études offertes à Barthélémy Mercadal*. Editions Francis Lefebre, 2002.

Saragoça, J.L. 'El nuevo régimen jurídico del contrato de transporte nacional de mercancias por carretera en Portugal: assunción de las reglas CMR'. *Actualidad jurídica del transporte por carretera: in memoriam F.M. Sánchez Gamborino*. Madrid: Fundación Francisco Corell, 2005.

Schelin, J. 'Methods of Interpreting the CMR Convention'. *Transportrecht* 25 (2002): 382–384.

Schindler, A. 'La nueva ley alemana de transportes de 1998 y su modelo: la Convención CMR'. *Actualidad jurídica del transporte por carretera: in memoriam F.M. Sánchez Gamborino*. Madrid: Fundación Francisco Corell, 2005.

Schlüter, A. 'Das Haftungssystem im Transportrecht: Individualvereinbarungen, AGB und zwingende CMR-Bestimmungen im grenzüberschreitenden Transport'. *Zivil- und Wirtschaftsrecht im europäischen und globalen Kontext* (2006): 537–556.

Schmid, R.T. 'Auswirkung der Transportrechtsreform auf die Anwendung der CMR durch deutsche Gerichte und höchstrichterliche Rechtsprechung in der Bundesrepublik Deutschland zu aktuellen Problemen der CMR'. *European Transport Law* 36 (2001): 737–750.

Shariatmadari, S.H. 'Die internationale Zuständigkeit bei Nichteinlassung des Beklagten zur Sache und die Einrede der Rechtshängigkeit bei negativer Feststellungsklage im Rahmen des Art. 31 CMR im Lichte der neueren Rechtsprechung des EuGH und des BGH'. *Transportrecht* 29 (2006): 105–109.

Smeele, F.G.M. 'Dutch Case Law on Art. 29 CMR [Belgisch-Nederlands CMR-Seminar, 26 mei 2000]'. *European Transport Law* 35 (2000–3): 329–341.

Smeele, F.G.M. 'Dutch Case Law on Art. 29 CMR Revisited'. *European Transport Law* 36 (2001): 37–40.

Thume, K.-H. 'Vergleich der Haftungsregeln des Warschauer Abkommens mit denen der CMR'. *Transportrecht* 19 (1996): 143.

Thume, K.-H. 'Aktivlegitimation und Regressverfolgung in Deutschland, dargestellt am Beispiel der CMR'. *European Transport Law* 40 (2005): 801–810.

Thume, K.-H. Aktivlegitimation und Regreßverfolgung in Deutschland dargestellt am Beispiel der CMR'. *Transportrecht* 28 (2005): 225–228.

Thume, K.H. (ed.). *Kommentar zur CMR*. 2. neu bearb. Aufl. Frankfurt am Main: Recht u. Wirtschaft, 2006, 1190 (RIW-Buch).

Thume, K.-H. 'Kosten des Vorprozesses bei Regehaftung des CMR-Frachtführers'. *Transportrecht* 35 (2012): 2, 61–63.

Thume, K.-H. 'Die CMR – Siegeszug eines internationalen Abkommens über drei Kontinente'. *Recht der internationalen Wirtschaft* 59 (2013): 4, 177.

Tilche, M. & P. Brunat. 'Transposition de la CMR. Adapter sans copier'. *Bulletin des transports et de la logistique* (2000), 175–176.

Tilche, M. 'Jurisprudencia francesa sobre la convención CMR: una interpretación nacional'. *Actualidad jurídica del transporte por carretera: in memoriam F.M. Sánchez Gamborino*. Madrid: Fundación Francisco Corell, 2005.

Tilche, M. 'Le jubilé de la CMR'. *Bulletin des transports et de la logistique* (2006): 335–338.

Tountopoulos, V.D. 'Die griechische Rechtsprechung zum Begriff des "wilful misconduct" des Frachtführers nach Art. 29 CMR'. *Transportrecht* 35 (2012): 7, 283–290.

Tuma, O.J. 'Ist grobe Fahrlässigkeit ein Tatbestand des Art. 29 CMR?'. *European Transport Law* 37 (2002): 139–166.

Van Acker, M. 'Beförderung durch aufeinanderfolgende FRACHTFÜHRER gemäß Art. 34 ff. CMR'. *European Transport Law* 36 (2001): 717–730.

Verbeke, L. 'Stuwing door de afzender in het wegvervoer: gedeelde aansprakelijkheid? [Belgisch-Nederlands CMR-Seminar, 26 mei 2000]'. *European Transport Law* 35 (2000–3): 313–327.

Verguts, P. 'De verhaalbaarheid van de BTW onder artikel 23, 4 CMR'. *European Transport Law* (2002): 479–496.

Viñal, A. 'El ámbito de aplicación del convenio relativo al contrato de transporte internacional de mercancías por carretera: el articulo 1 del Convenio CMR'. *Actualidad jurídica del transporte por carretera: in memoriam F.M. Sánchez Gamborino*. Madrid: Fundación Francisco Corell, 2005.

Wijffels, R. 'Introduction to the CMR with Regard to Linguistic Inaccuracies'. *European Transport Law* 36 (2001): 653–657.

Wijffels, R. 'Uniformización y desuniformización del derecho del transporte por carretera: El art. 29 de la convención CMR y otros factores'. *Actualidad jurídica del transporte por carretera: in memoriam F.M. Sánchez Gamborino*. Madrid: Fundación Francisco Corell, 2005.

Windahl, J. 'Mere om regres mellem CMR-fragtførere'. *Ugeskrift for Retsvæsen* (2001), Litterær afdeling, 391–396.

Zapp, M. 'Der Schadensersatzanspruch des Empfängers gemäß Art. 13 CMR'. *Liber Amicorum Robert Wijffels*, edited by M.-P. Serck. Antwerpen: ETL, 2001.

Cultural Property

Advisory Panel on Illicit Trade 'Report of the Advisory Panel on Illicit Trade' [appointed by the Rt Hon Alan Howarth CBE, Minister for the Arts ... under the chairmanship of Normal Palmer, Barrister, Professor of Commercial Law at University College London], *Art, Antiquity and Law* 6 (2001): 65–98.

Bergé, J.-S. 'La Convention d'UNIDROIT sur les biens culturels: remarques sur la dynamique des sources en droit international'. *Journal du droit international* 127 (2000): 215–262.

Bergé, J.-S. 'La Convention d'UNIDROIT sur les biens culturels retour sur un texte majeur dans la lutte contre un fait international illicite de circulation'. 20 *Uniform Law Review* (2015).

Blake, J. 'On Defining the Cultural Heritage'. *International and Comparative Law Quarterly* 49 (2000): 61–85.

Calvo Caravaca, A.-L. 'Private International Law and the UNIDROIT Convention of 24th June 1995 on Stolen or Illegally Exported Cultural Objects'. In *Festschrift für Erik Jayme*, edited by H.-P. Mansel et al. München: Sellier European Law Publishers, 2004.

Calvo Caravaca, A.-L. 'El convenio di UNIDROIT de 24 junio de 1995'. *La protección jurídico internacional del patrimonio cultural* (2009): 155–189.

Carducci, G. 'Complémentarité entre les Conventions de l'UNESCO de 1970 et d'UNIDROIT de 1995 sur les biens culturels'. *Uniform Law Review* 11 (2006): 93–102.

Carruthers, J.M. 'Cultural Property and Law – An International Private Law Perspective'. *Juridical Review* (2001): 127–145.

Selected Bibliography

Celso Da Silva, O. 'Breve notícia sobre a ratificação pelo Brasil da Convenção da UNIDROIT sobra bens culturais furtados ou ilicitamente exportados, concluída em Roma, em 24 junho de 1995'. *Revista de Direito do Mercosul* 4 (2000): 37–43.

Cornu, E. & B. Elster. 'Quelle protection pour l'objet d'art lors de sa vente ou de son exportation?'. *Journal des tribunaux* 119 (2000): 455–459.

Coulee, F. 'Quelques remarques sur la restitution interétatique des biens culturels sous l'angle du droit international public'. *Revue générale de droit international public* (2000): 358–392.

Di Maio, F. 'La Convenzione UNIDROIT, la direttiva 93/7/CEE e l'azione coordinata delle forze di polizia'. *La circolazione illecita delle opere d'arte. Principio della buona fede. Atti del 6° Convegno Internazionale patrocinato dalla Commissione Europea e dal Ministero per i Beni e le Attività Culturali, Bollettino di Numismatica*, Supplemento al 36 (2001): 155–156.

Estrella Faria, J.A. 'UNESCO, UNIDROIT und Kulturgüterschutz'. *Bulletin Kunst und Recht*, 2 (2014), pp. 5–18.

Estrella Faria, J.A. 'UNESCO, UNIDROIT y la restitución de bienes culturales'. *La convención de la UNESCO de 1970*, 2013, pp. 19–33.

Frigo, M. 'La Convenzione dell'UNIDROIT sui beni culturali rubati o illecitamente esportati'. *Rivista di Diritto Internazionale Privato e Processuale* 32 (1996): 435.

Frigo, M. *La circolazione internazionale dei beni culturali. Diritto internazionale, diritto comunitario e diritto interno*. Milano: Giuffrè Editore, 2001, 341. (*L'Italia e la vita giuridica internazionale. Collana di testi, casi, documenti diretta da Fausto Pocar*, 18).

Frigo, M. 'The Impact of the UNIDROIT Convention on the International Case-Law and Practice: An Appraisal'. 20 *Uniform Law Review* (2015).

Gatti, E. 'Commercializzazione illecita delle opere d'arte e principio della buona fede. Riflessioni sulle rispettive legislazioni nazionali alla luce della Direttiva Comunitaria 93/7/CEE e della Convenzione UNIDROIT'. *La circolazione illecita delle opere d'arte. Principio della buona fede. Atti del 6° Convegno Internazionale patrocinato dalla Commissione Europea e dal Ministero per i Beni e le Attività Culturali, Bollettino di Numismatica*, Supplemento al 36 (2001): 313–320.

Gill, D. 'From Boston to Rome: Reflections on Returning Antiquities'. *International Journal of Cultural Property* 13 (2006): 311–331.

Gonzalez Campos, J. 'La loi applicable au transfert de la propriété des biens culturels: spécialisation et matérialisation des règles du droit international privé'. *Estudos em homenagem à Professora Doutora Isabel de Magalhães Collaço*, edited by R.M. Moura Ramos et al. Coimbra: Almedina, 2002.

Guss, A. 'International Conference The 1995 UNIDROIT Convention: Cultural objects of the crossroad of rights and interest to celebrate the 25th anniversary of the 1995 UNIDROIT Convention on Stolen or Illegally Exported Cultural Objects, 8–9 October 2020, Rome. 2021 *Cultural Heritage Law*. 293–299.

Halsdorfer, A. 'Sollte Deutschland dem UNIDROIT-Kulturgutübereinkommen 1995 beitreten?'. *IPRax* 29 (2009): 307–311.

Jouanny, J.P. 'La Convenzione UNIDROIT del 1995 e l'attività dell'O.I.P.C. – Interpol'. *La circolazione illecita delle opere d'arte. Principio della buona fede.* Atti del 6° Convegno Internazionale patrocinato dalla Commissione Europea e dal Ministero per i Beni e le Attività Culturali, Bollettino di Numismatica, Supplemental 36 (2001): 103–112.

Kaliampestsos, I. 'UNESCO-UNIDROIT: praktische Erfahrungen aus Griechenland'. *Bulletin Kunst und Recht*, 2 (2014), pp. 25–35.

Kohls, F. *Kulturgüterschutz*, Frankfurt a. M.: Peter Lang, 2001 (*Europäische Hochschulschriften. Reihe 2, Rechtswissenschaft*, vol. 3191).

Kosmopoulos, A.M. 'Traffico illecito di beni culturali: principio della buona fede. Riflessioni sulle leggi nazionali alla luce della Direttiva Comunitaria e della Convenzione UNIDROIT'. *La circolazione illecita delle opere d'arte. Principio della buona fede. Atti del 6° Convegno Internazionale patrocinato dalla Commissione Europea e dal Ministero per i Beni e le Attività Culturali*, Bollettino di Numismatica, Supplemento al 36 (2001): 41–46.

Lagarde, P. 'La restitution internationale des biens culturels en dehors de la Convention de l'UNESCO de 1970 et de la Convention d'UNIDROIT de 1995'. *Uniform Law Review* 11 (2006): 83–91.

Lagiewska, M. 'Ratification of the 1995 UNIDROIT Convention in Poland: Pipe dream or realistic prospect?' 2021 *Cultural Heritage Law*. 125–133.

Magri, G. 'A survey of the 1970 UNESCO and 1995 UNIDROIT Conventions and their effects on Italian and European private law. 2021 *Cultural Heritage Law*, 110–124.

Martynenka, I. 'Public Order and the Protection of Cultural Heritage: Enforcement of UNESCO and UNIDROIT Conventions in CIS Countries'. *Public Policy and Ordre public* 3 (2012): 39–61.

Merryman, J.H. 'Cultural Property Trade Law in the Third Millenium'. *Rivista del Diritto Commerciale* 98 (2000): Pt. I, 385–402.

Miller, D.L.C., D.W. Meyers & A.L.Cowe. 'Restitution of Art and Cultural Objects: A Re-assessment of the Role of Limitation'. *Art, Antiquity and Law* 6 (2001): 1–17.

Nafziger, J.A.R. 'Towards a More Collaborative Regime of Transnational Cultural Property Law'. *Private Law in the International Arena. From National Conflict Rules Towards Harmonization and Unification. Liber Amicorum Kurt Siehr*. Zürich: T.M.C. Asser Press, Schulthess, 2000.

Panone, F. 'INTERPOL's Position on the 1970 and 1995 Conventions Governing the International Circulation of Cultural Property' 20 *Uniform Law Review* (2015).

Prott, L.V. 'Cultural Heritage Law: The Perspective of the Source Nations'. *Art, Antiquity and Law* 4 (2000): 333–342.

Prott, L.V. *Biens culturels volés ou illicitement exportés. Commentaire relatif à la Convention d'UNIDROIT (1995)*. Paris: UNESCO, 2000.

Prott, L. 'The UNIDROIT Convention on Stolen or Illegally Exported Cultural Objects – Ten Years On'. *Uniform Law Review* (2009): 215–237.

Prott, L.V., Adlercreutz, T. 'Commentary on the UNIDROIT Convention on stolen and illegally exported cultural objects 1995: return and restitution in the 21st century', Leicester: *Inst. of Art and Law*, 2021, xxi-160.

Rahmaoui, K. 'Protection internationale des biens culturels: faut-il adhérer à la Convention d'UNIDROIT?'. El Acil (4 January 2000): 10.

Rau, M. 'Kulturgüterschutz im Meer: eine erste Analyse der neuen UNESCO-Konvention'. *Zeitschrift für ausländisches öffentliches Recht und Völkerrecht* 61 (2001): 833–876.

Reichelt, G. 'UNESCO-UNIDROIT-Internationaler Kulturgüterschutz'. *Bulletin Kunst und Recht*, 2 (2014), pp. 48–56.

Rodinò, W. 'La Convenzione UNIDROIT sui beni culturali rubati o illecitamente esportati'. *Protezione internazionale del patrimonio culturale: interessi nazionali e difesa del patrimonio comune della cultura. Atti del Convegno, Roma, 8–9 maggio 1998*, 103–118. A cura di F. Francioni, A. Del Vecchio, P. De Caterini. Milano: Giuffrè Editore, 2000.

Roodt, C. 'Cultural Heritage Jurisprudence and Strategies for Retention and Recovery'. *The Comparative and International Law Journal of Southern Africa* 35 (2002): 157–181.

Sánchez Cordero Davila, J.A. 'Les biens culturels précolombiens' (*Bibliothèque de droit privé*, 404). Paris: L.G.D.J., 2004, 476.

Sánchez Cordero Davila, J.A. The Private Art Collections. 20 *Uniform Law Review* (2015).

Schneider, M. 'La Convenzione UNIDROIT e il principio della buona fede'. *La circolazione illecita delle opere d'arte. Principio della buona fede. Atti del 6° Convegno Internazionale patrocinato dalla Commissione Europea e dal Ministero per i Beni e le Attività Culturali, Bollettino di Numismatica*, Supplemento al 36 (2001): 85–102.

Shyllon, F. 'The Recovery of Cultural Objects by African States Through the UNESCO and UNIDROIT Conventions and the Role of Arbitration'. *Uniform Law Review* (2000): 219–241.

Siehr, K. 'Das UNIDROIT-Übereinkommen von 1995 und Staatseigentum an archäologischen Kulturgütern'. *Problemi e tendenze del diritto internazionale dell'economia* (2011), 983–997.

Siehr, K. 'UNIDROIT Convention of 1995 and unclaimed cultural property without provenance'. *ELTE Law Journal*, (2014) 1, pp. 89–102.

Silva Neto, O. Celso da. 'Breve noticia sobre a ratificação pelo Brasil da Convenção da UNIDROIT sobre bens culturais furtados ou ilicitamente exportados, concluida em Roma, em 24 de junho de 1995'. *Revista de derecho internacional y del Mercosur/Revista de Direito Internacional e do Mercosul* 6, no. 3 (2002): 35–40.

Struell, F.D. 'Some Remarks on a New Joint Project of the American Law Institute and UNIDROIT'. *The International Lawyer* 34 (2000): 1071–1086.

Thorn, B. *Internationaler Kulturgüterschutz nach der UNIDROIT-Konvention* (*Schriften zum Kulturgüterschutz* / Cultural Property Studies). Berlin: De Gruyter, 2005.

Turner, S. *Das Restitutionsrecht des Staates nach illegaler Ausfuhr von Kulturgütern. Eigentumsordnung und völkerrechtliche Zuordnung*. (*Schriften zum Kulturgüterschutz*) Berlin, New York: Walter de Gruyter, 2002.

UNIDROIT 'UNIDROIT Convention on Stolen or Illegally Exported Cultural Objects: Explanatory report' [in English and in French]. *Uniform Law Review* 6 (2001): 476–581.

Van Woudenberg, N. 'Adherence to the 1995 UNIDROIT Convention: wider than one would think at first sight', in: *Uniform Law Review*, 21 (2016) 1, pp. 120–128.

Vrellis. S. 'Les biens archéologiques et la Convention d'UNIDROIT (1995) sur les biens culturels volés ou illicitement exportés'. 20 *Uniform Law Review* (2015).

Walden, D.A. 'Working "Without" UNIDROIT: A Canadian Perspective'. *Art, Antiquity and Law* 7 (2002): 55–63.

Yatsunami, R. 'A methodological consideration on internationa trafficking of cultural property: an approach from Bayesian statistics, 2021 *Cultural Heritage Law*, 28–46.

Selected Bibliography

Index

The numbers here refer to paragraph numbers. Some of the paragraph numbers accompany with footnote numer (fn).

Index

Index

Index

www.ingramcontent.com/pod-product-compliance
Lightning Source LLC
LaVergne TN
LVHW011134300926
849160LV00008B/641